34⁰⁰

HD 31 .B633 2000
Boulmetis, John.
The ABC's of evaluation

The ABCs of Evaluation

The ABCs of Evaluation

Timeless Techniques for Program and Project Managers

John Boulmetis
Phyllis Dutwin

JOSSEY-BASS
A Wiley Imprint
www.josseybass.com

Published by Jossey-Bass
A Wiley Imprint
989 Market Street, San Francisco, CA 94103-1741   www.josseybass.com

Jossey-Bass books and products are available through most bookstores. To contact Jossey-Bass directly
call our Customer Care Department within the U.S. at 800-956-7739, outside the U.S. at 317-572-3986
or fax 317-572-4002.

Jossey-Bass also publishes its books in a variety of electronic formats. Some content that appears in
print may not be available in electronic books.

The list of the four levels of evaluation on p. 9 is reprinted with permission of the publisher. From
Evaluating Training Programs, copyright © 1994 by D. L. Kirkpatrick, Barrett-Koehler Publishers, Inc.,
San Francisco, CA. All rights reserved. 1-800-929-2929.

"An Evaluator's Program Description Dialogue" in Chapter Four is adapted from An Evaluation Primer
Workbook: Practical Exercises for the Health Professional by A. Fink and J. Kosecoff, copyright © 1978
by Sage Publications, Inc. Reprinted by permission of Sage Publications, Inc.

Library of Congress Cataloging-in-Publication Data

Boulmetis, John.
    The ABCs of evaluation : timeless techniques for program and
project managers / John Boulmetis, Phyllis Dutwin. — 1st ed.
    p.   cm.
    Includes bibliographical references (p.   ) and index.
    ISBN 0-7879-4432-7 (hard : perm. paper)
    1. Management—Evaluation. I. Dutwin, Phyllis. II. Title.
    HD31 .B633   1998
    658.4'032—dc21
                                                          99-6597

Printed in the United States of America

FIRST EDITION
HB Printing   10 9 8 7 6 5 4 3

Contents

Preface   ix

The Authors   xv

1. What Is Evaluation?   1

2. Why Evaluate?   22

3. Decision Making: Whom to Involve, How, and Why?   33

4. Starting Point: The Evaluator's Program Description   54

5. Choosing an Evaluation Model   67

6. Data Sources   85

7. Data Analysis   107

8. Is It Evaluation or Is It Research?   125

9. Writing the Evaluation Report   139

Appendix: More on Data Analysis   155

Sample Evaluation Report   165

References   201

Index   203

Preface

Evaluation is a task that every program and project manager will face at one time or another: you may manage the funding process for an organization, or direct a self-study that requires evaluation, or write a grant proposal that includes an evaluation segment. Occasions vary, but they are inevitable.

Still, endorsing evaluation is a lot like endorsing regular visits to the dentist. People are quick to endorse both activities, but when it comes to doing either one, most people are very uncomfortable. *The ABCs of Evaluation* will reduce your discomfort by doing two things: First, the book will demystify the process of designing and conducting an evaluation by helping you understand the components of an evaluation design. Second, and more important, the book's aim is to convince you that *you* play an integral part in any evaluation process, and therefore *you* are a beneficiary of the results.

Who is the *you* that this book is designed to assist in the process of evaluation? You might be a manager, supervisor, team facilitator, analyst, or evaluator in the private sector. Then again, you might be in the public or private sector as an administrator, coordinator, facilitator, consultant, or evaluator. Or you might be a faculty member or student in any of a host of disciplines (education, management, human services, psychology, public affairs, labor relations or health). For any of these situations, the book will provide you with a basic understanding of the steps to follow to design, conduct, and supervise a program evaluation.

This volume has been designed to serve as an introduction to evaluation for program and project managers who have little experience in this task. It presents time-tested evaluation principles and techniques, but it does not purport to reflect the totality of the professional field of evaluation, which encompasses a far greater range of techniques and technologies than are suited to the needs and interests of this book's readership.

Demonstrating Success

As a professional, you know that your programs need to show evidence of success. For example, regardless of how important a communication skills training seminar might be to the overall team-building effort of a company, if you cannot show how it affected the employees' teamwork skills or how improved teamwork added to company performance, the program might not be funded again. This realization may have originated with you, or the organization may require evaluations and demand accountability. If you have always assumed that evaluations are just too difficult for you to do, that you don't want to tackle difficult data collection or unfathomable data analysis, think again. *The ABCs of Evaluation* will dispel these misconceptions and show you what to do.

Both the person who is designing and performing an evaluation and the person who is participating in and receiving the findings of an evaluation need to prepare themselves to understand the basic processes involved. The evaluator, by understanding the thoughts, concerns, and questions of the evaluated, can better anticipate and prepare to address them up front. The evaluated, by anticipating the processes, the probing, and the data requests of an evaluator, can position themselves to make better use of the evaluation process and results.

Too often people feel that evaluation is something that is done *to* them rather than *for* them. Indeed, evaluation may be seen as something to get through and get around (Gray, 1998).

The ABCs of Evaluation is an easy-to-read explanation of the concepts and methods of the evaluation process. The chapters are designed to teach readers what the process offers, what it consists of, and how it is designed and implemented. In addition, the book will guide managers step-by-step throughout the process of conducting an evaluation, from the early question, "Why evaluate?" to the later one, "What did the evaluation tell me?" Consequently, the book will be useful to those who design and conduct the evaluation, as well as to those who supervise others in these tasks.

You may be experiencing downsizing, reorganization, or the introduction of high-performance work teams where you work. These new circumstances may require you to possess evaluation skills. Although you now find yourself in a position that requires the skills, you may not have them, or you may not have been trained to use them.

Overview

At the beginning of each chapter, a scenario sets the stage. Then the chapter presents new evaluation concepts followed by concluding exercises designed to challenge your understanding.

Chapter One defines evaluation, keeping in mind that it is considered both an art and a science. The chapter proposes that readers learn principles and theories as a first step and then apply them in actual situations.

In Chapter One, you will learn that evaluation, both quantitative and qualitative, means measuring and collecting data against some standard. The evaluation may be of people, any activity, an entire program, or all of the above.

After an introduction to the formal reasons to evaluate (more on this in Chapter Two), the chapter explores the ideas of setting standards, using project cycles, and determining levels in evaluation.

Finally, there is an introduction to the evaluation design format that the reader will learn to use throughout the book.

Chapter Two encourages you to think about the following: where there is a program, there must be evaluation. The "Why?" of evaluation emanates from different sources or audiences—from a need you have, or from a requirement that administration or management has for planning, policymaking, funding, or ongoing research. Whatever its purposes and objectives, evaluation is an integral part of most programs and should be planned from the outset. The evaluation design format introduced in Chapter One comes into use here to address your need to define your audience and to eventually report to that audience.

Chapter Three explores the importance of management buy-in to decision making and explores how staff, subject-matter experts, and other stakeholders are involved in the preplanning, planning, and application of the evaluation. The chapter also addresses this question: How can I evaluate a program I did not help create?

Evaluation decisions flow through the various stages in the evaluation. Consequently, in this chapter you will learn whom to involve in the evaluation, and how and why they should be involved. You will learn how to monitor evaluation data and engage in process (formative) evaluation as well as product (summative) evaluation.

Chapter Four addresses a number of questions regarding the evaluator's program description: Why do you need it? How does it relate to your objectives and activities? The chapter will include discussion of the importance of gleaning information from program staff, for example, goals and objectives, the activities planned to achieve the goals and objectives, and the measures that will be used to evaluate the results. The discussion may also involve more than one level of goals and objectives, such as those of the organization, the staff members, and the clients.

The purpose of Chapter Five is to describe different models of evaluation and to illustrate the circumstances under which each is used. Certain design components are shared by all models: evaluation questions, activities to observe, data sources, whom you collect data from or about, how and when you collect the data, how you analyze the data, and who is responsible for each piece of the evaluation.

In Chapter Six, you will learn to identify the data sources that will help you, as an evaluator, to determine whether the program has met its objectives. Two important questions are answered: How do data sources relate to the evaluator's program description? Are paper-and-pencil instruments the only form of measurement?

Chapter Six discusses many forms of data collection, among them using existing data, such as previously collected public records, and collecting new data using surveys, checklists, interview schedules, objective tests and scales, projective measures, and observational analysis.

Chapter Six also differentiates between data collection formats that are obtrusive (when people know you are collecting information) and those that are unobtrusive (when people are unaware that you are collecting information).

In Chapter Seven, data analysis will become an understandable concept for you. Specifically, Chapter Seven introduces data analysis by levels of measurement: nominal, ordinal, interval, and ratio. Data analysis terms such as *measures of central tendency* and *analysis of variance*, which are ways of analyzing differences (growth and change), are discussed by level.

The purpose of Chapter Eight is to help you distinguish between evaluation and research. The chapter discusses both quantitative and qualitative approaches. You will also learn the essential facts about samples, including why you would use sampling, what the various sampling terms mean, and what you need to know about sample size. These questions and others are answered in very clear language: What are control and experimental groups? Is it always possible to have these in your evaluation? When is it possible, and when is it not? The chapter also addresses how you deal with nonresponse.

Chapter Nine, Writing the Evaluation Report, has its basis in Chapter Three's learning about the program's stakeholders. All or any of the stakeholders might receive the report. The chapter reviews your audiences: clients, program staff, organization, or sponsor. In addition, the chapter suggests the many possibilities for focus in the report. As the report writer, you may focus on any or all of the following points: philosophy and goals of the organization, client, community; the needs assessment; program planning; program implementation; and evaluation. Chapter Nine suggests an outline that an evaluator can adopt or adapt for his or her own report.

The Appendix, More on Data Analysis, is included for those readers who wish to delve further into the specifics of data analysis.

Finally, we present a sample evaluation report that has been annotated to illustrate the concepts in this book.

Using This Book

The ABCs of Evaluation is applicable to all sectors of the organizational world (that is, business, education, community-based organizations, the health sector, the public sector) rather than focusing on any one sector. Note that the book will not provide specific instructions on designing personnel appraisals. However, by becoming familiar with the basic steps in the evaluation process, following the scenarios provided in each chapter, and using the additional resources at the end of each chapter, the reader should become considerably more comfortable with the evaluation process. The novice evaluator will find it an invaluable guide leading to yet more lessons that can only be learned through the experience of conducting both internal and external evaluations.

Depending on your level of experience, knowledge, or comfort with the evaluation processes, you may wish to cover the entire text in a stepwise progression or use parts of it to complete and complement what you already know. Whatever the case, *The ABCs of Evaluation* can take on the role of primer for the novice evaluator or resource for the seasoned evaluator.

The Authors

John Boulmetis is professor in the School of Education and coordinator of the graduate program in Adult Education at the University of Rhode Island. Since 1985 he has also been director of URI's Institute of Human Science and Services. Boulmetis received his master's degree in education from the University of Rhode Island, and his doctoral degree in vocational education from Ohio State University. During the past twenty-six years, Dr. Boulmetis has been consultant to public and private institutions for the purposes of training, training development, third-party evaluation, and program planning. He has assisted in the development, operation, and conduct of a national study of competency-based adult vocational programs in the U.S., and has been principal investigator on projects dealing with evaluation, needs assessment, curriculum development, and human services agencies in the states of Rhode Island and Connecticut. A member of the American Association of Adult and Continuing Education, the American Vocational Association, and the Rhode Island Association of Adult and Continuing Education, Boulmetis was honored in 1987 by the Rhode Island Association of Adult and Continuing Education as the Rhode Island Adult Educator of the Year. He is the author of numerous keynote addresses at national and international conferences, evaluation reports, articles, and books, including *Job Competency: Adult Vocational Instruction* (1981).

Phyllis Dutwin is president of Dutwin Associates, a training and development firm, and former vice president of Reading and Educational Services of New Jersey. She received her master's degree in adult education, training, and development from the University of Rhode Island. Dutwin consults with major publishers to develop and write books that help students and adults advance their personal and workplace skills, and has also consulted with the State Department of Education in New Jersey, Texas Instruments, and Textron Chamber of Commerce School in Providence, Rhode Island. An adult educator with more than twenty years of experience in designing reading, writing, and ESL programs, as well as in teaching adults in corporate, classroom, and individual settings, she was honored, in 1993, for her outstanding contributions to the Adult Educators of New England. Dutwin is a member of the American Association of Training and Development, the American Association for Adult and Continuing Education, and the Rhode Island Literacy Adult Council. Among her books are *English the Easy Way*, 3rd ed. (1996), *Read to Work: Business Occupations* (1999), *Read to Work: Health Occupations* (1999), and *Writing the Easy Way: For School, Business, and Personal Situations*, 3rd ed. (2000).

1

What Is Evaluation?

SCENARIO ONE   The administration at Grandview Retirement and Nursing Facility strongly promotes ongoing education and training for all staff. In fact, when personnel are hired, they agree to take two courses each year, selected from a long list of possible courses decided upon by administration and staff. Topics are many and diverse, from the law and patient rights, to medication in geriatric care, to the mind-body connection. Two of the recent training programs were devoted to answering these questions: (1) Is there a connection between mental and physical activity and sustained good health and longevity? (2) How do you encourage residents to stay both mentally and physically active? The staff, both program and nursing, found the answer to the first question—that activity is indeed linked to well-being and longevity—compelling (Wells, 1997). They decided to institute additional programs for residents that would involve both mental and physical activity.

Coincidentally, a volunteer had been coming to the retirement and nursing facility for about six months to work with interested residents in an informal gardening program. The volunteer, Ruth, discovered that one of the things the residents missed very much when they left their homes was their gardening. The activity helped them regain what they had enjoyed and gave them a real opportunity for mental and physical engagement. The facility had a limited budget, so Ruth made her own in-kind donations.

From the beginning, however, the activity was extremely popular and she knew that available resources would not be sufficient to serve all the people who wanted to take part in the program. Ruth volunteered to look for funds, a grant that would allow Grandview to continue and enlarge the program. The administrators said they would be delighted if she would do the legwork, but of course they would need to know exactly what she was doing along the way so that they could keep their board of directors apprised.

Not long after this, Ruth discovered that the Cox Foundation funded this kind of program and she got their grant application. One of the first items that she read on the application asked for an evaluation of the program. The items in the evaluation question included listing program objectives (for example, to increase residents' activity and mobility level) and listing measurements (both quantitative and qualitative) that would be used as indicators of achievement of those objectives. Ruth later learned that a quantitative measure might be the number of times residents took part in the gardening activities before the onset of the funded program compared to the end of the program. A qualitative measure might be perceptions of garden activity staff regarding the focus and mood of residents.

The grant also called for explaining data collection methods, a discussion of any sampling that would be done, a description of the evaluation design, the data analysis that would occur, the staffing, and the final report.

Although she was puzzled about most of the items, Ruth hoped that subsequent meetings and discussions with the staff would answer her questions. She needed some basic questions answered first: Why do programs need to be evaluated? What is evaluation? What are you looking for when you evaluate a program? How is this different from research?

Unlike Ruth, readers of this book will not have to wait to have these questions answered. They just need to read Chapter One. After reading this chapter, readers should be able to answer the following questions as they relate to the preceding scenario as well as to the chapter material.

1. What do all evaluations have in common?
2. How would you characterize the differences in the efficiency, effectiveness, and impact of a program?
3. Why evaluate in the first place?

Key Words and Concepts

Efficiency: The degree to which a program or project has been productive in relationship to its resources

Effectiveness: The degree to which goals have been reached

Impact: The degree to which a program or project resulted in changes

Common Denominators

Before we embark on a definition of evaluation, we need to answer the volunteer's question. How does program evaluation differ from research? Unlike evaluation, research takes place in a precisely controlled environment. The Grandview gardening program could not comply with this definition. Among a number of other important reasons that we will discuss in Chapters Five and Eight, Grandview's project staff could not precisely control (nor would they want to) the number and choice of participants. In addition, research collects data to stretch the envelope of what is known in order to prove or disprove a hypothesis or presupposition. Evaluation looks at program and project objectives and asks whether they have been achieved, judges the worth of ongoing programs, decides upon the usefulness of new programs or projects, and so forth (Rossi and Freeman, 1993).

In both for-profit and nonprofit organizations, managers possess data (information) that could help to evaluate a program or project. These data are the one thing that all evaluations have in common regardless of the particular definition of evaluation one embraces: evaluation is the systematic process of collecting data that help identify the strengths and weaknesses of a program or project. The data may be as simple as records of attendance at training sessions or as complex as test scores showing the impact of a new educational program on increasing students' knowledge across an entire school system.

Whatever definition you apply to evaluation, when your task is to perform a program evaluation you will almost certainly include a number of common evaluation steps. You will find these listed as program cycles in the Putting It All Together section later in this chapter.

Two Definitions of Evaluation

People do not always agree on one definition of evaluation. Following are statements that reflect two different definitions:

- Evaluation is the systematic process of collecting and analyzing data in order to determine whether and to what degree objectives have been or are being achieved.
- Evaluation is the systematic process of collecting and analyzing data in order to make a decision.

Notice that the first ten words in each of the definitions are the same. However, the reasons—the "Why?"—for collecting and analyzing the data reflect a notable difference in the philosophies behind each definition. The first reflects a philosophy that as an evaluator, you are interested in knowing only if something worked, if it was effective in doing what it was supposed to do. The second statement reflects the philosophy that evaluation makes claims on the value of something in relation to the overall operation of a program, project, or event. Indeed, many experts agree that an evaluation should not only assess program results but also identify ways to improve the program evaluated (Wholey, Hatry, and Newcomer, 1994). A program may be effective but of limited value to the client or sponsor. One can imagine, however, using an evaluation to make a decision (the second definition) even if a program has reached its objectives (the first definition). Federal grants are based on the first statement, that is, whether the program has achieved its objectives, but the harder decision to downsize or change may be a consequence of the second definition of evaluation.

Evaluating Efficiency, Effectiveness, and Impact

We can define evaluation even more closely as a process. The process is guided by the reason for doing the evaluation in the first place. An evaluation might be a process of examining a training program, in light of values or standards, for the purpose of making certain decisions about the *efficiency*, *effectiveness*, or *impact* of the program. To carry out this task, you need to understand the concepts of efficiency, effectiveness, and impact. These three terms will be referred to from this point on as the levels of program evaluation. (See Table 1.1 later in this chapter.)

Efficiency relates to an analysis of the costs (dollars, people, time, facilities, materials, and so forth) that are expended as part of a program in comparison to either their benefits or effectiveness. How is efficiency, or the competence with which a program is carried out, measured in a program? The term itself gives clues to what this is about. Program monitors look at the efficiency with which details are carried out in a program. Programs often begin with recruiting, gathering materials, providing for space, setting up fiscal procedures, and so forth. Thus the relationship between the costs and end products becomes the focus of an efficiency evaluation. Although very important, these aspects of efficiency may have no bearing on the program's effectiveness. If the investment in the program or project exceeds the returns, there may be little or no efficiency.

For example, let's consider a nuclear power facility that houses a rather substantial training and staff development enterprise. As part of this enterprise, ten instructors are responsible for ensuring that five hundred employees are cycled through training every six months, for a minimum of twenty hours of training each cycle. The training revisits the employees' basic knowledge of their job and introduces new concepts developed since the last training. The staff development enterprise might work very efficiently by making sure that all employees cycle through in a timely fashion, in small enough groups to utilize the best of what we know about how adults learn. The students' time on task is often not enough, however, and many of them do not retain much of what was covered in the training. Thus the program is not effective.

The enterprise may be efficient in that it fully utilized the time of each of the available trainers, it stayed within the parameters of the staff development budget, it kept employee "down time" to a minimum, it used materials and equipment that were available, and it completed the training agenda for the company. Yet there may be an increase in accidents or hazardous incidents because of employees making simple, basic mistakes. The enterprise's training was efficient but not necessarily effective.

When you look at the effectiveness of your program, you are asking this question: "Did the activities do what they were supposed to do?" Simply put, a program's effectiveness is measured in terms of substantive changes in knowledge, attitudes, or skills on the part of a program's clients. Although the right number of participants may have been recruited and the best possible site may have been secured, the effectiveness test is this: Did the activities provide the skills to run the new equipment? Did the participants gain the knowledge they need to sell the new mortgage or other banking product?

In another example, the same nuclear power staff development program may conduct a training session on a new procedure to decontaminate after entering a containment area. The trainer may pretest all the employees as they begin their training session. Upon completion, the employees are posttested and the results compared to determine whether their knowledge increased, decreased, or stayed the same. An increase in their knowledge would be an indication that the training was effective—it did what it was supposed to do. Yet two weeks after the training, when one of the employees was back at her job post, a situation arose in which she exited a hazardous area after spending some time checking water flow. She used the older, more comfortable procedure for decontamination and caused a problem that put her and her coworkers at risk. Here is an example of training that was effective—the worker passed all the posttests—but had little impact on changing the behavior of the employee.

Thus the impact that the program has had on the people or organization for which it was planned becomes an important evaluation consideration. Impact evaluation examines whether and to what extent there are long-term and sustained changes in a target population. Has the program or project brought about these desired changes? Are employees using the new procedures? And in other scenarios: Are more people off welfare? Has the program changed a family's life? Do your employees have more job satisfaction?

Evaluators frequently pay too little attention to assessing impact. One reason is that impacts often manifest themselves over time, and program managers have already turned their attention elsewhere before computing this aspect of the evaluation. The actual impact that training in new procedures might have in people's everyday life often needs time to percolate and evolve. An attempt to collect impact data after allowing for this delay may run into a number of blocks, such as learner turnover (you cannot find them), job or circumstance change (they no longer need to use the skills), or lack of time or resources for the evaluator to conduct these follow-up activities.

Still, program and project sponsors are most interested in impacts. Whether a learner feels satisfied with the training or the training results in knowledge gain means little to a sponsor or employer if the learning doesn't help the organization.

Evaluating Alternatives

The second philosophical statement that defines evaluation presents it as the process of delineating, obtaining, and providing useful information for the purpose of selecting among alternatives. Thus, it may not matter whether the program was efficiently conducted, effective, or had an impact on behavior or functions. Instead, the value of the evaluation is in its being able to compare one activity to another, one program to another, or one employee to another so that decisions can be made in the presence of empirically collected data. Search committees perform this kind of evaluation. In the course of their work, they describe job candidates' strengths, outline previous experiences, and acquire other useful information that makes it possible to choose among a number of candidates. A company planning to adopt and purchase a computer system will perform this kind of evaluation on all the systems it is considering. It will select the one that performs the best given the needs and resources of the company.

Identifying Areas to Improve

Finally, there is a third way of defining evaluation: Evaluation is the identification of discrepancies between where a program is currently and where it would like to be. For example, an organization's marketing department may have as one of its goals at least one face-to-face visit with customers per year. Currently, its sales force sees fewer than half the customers in a year. Records of face-to-face calls indicate the discrepancy between where XYZ Corporation is currently as opposed to where the organization wants to be.

Personnel evaluations often take on this definition as well. A new employee's first evaluation may be an example of the first definition, that is, an evaluation against some minimal standard of performance. After this initial evaluation, certain performance goals are set for the employee (either mutually or by the supervisor or team). The next and all the subsequent evaluations of that employee are compared with those performance goals or standards. The discrepancies are identified and remediation strategies are developed.

Other Levels

There are other levels of evaluation as defined by Kirkpatrick (1994). These levels refer to the eventual use of the evaluation data and who might make use of the results. Kirkpatrick's four levels of evaluation are as follows:

Level One: Participant impressions

Level Two: Effectiveness of the program

Level Three: Impact on the participants

Level Four: Return on investment for the organization (company, agency, or school system)

In level one you would be examining the perceptions of individuals who were directly involved as clients of your program. You would be interested in their perceptions of how they benefited from the program, what they thought of the program activities, and how they might use what they gained from the program. Program staff would be particularly interested in this level because the information would tell them how their efforts are being perceived and used.

In level two you would be measuring the effectiveness of the program in doing what it said it was going to do. There would be some comparison between a set of standards (criteria, goals or objectives) and what actually resulted. You might perform pretesting and posttesting of clients to ascertain their change, or compare one group who received the activities of the program with a group who did not to see the benefits of program participation. Program staff and sponsors would be particularly interested in the results of this level of evaluation.

In level three you would be attempting to discover the overall impact that the program had on clients: Did the program change their long-term behavior, attitudes, or performance? Were the changes observed in the level two evaluation sustainable over time? Sponsors, program staff, and clients would be interested in this level of evaluation.

In level four you would be determining the extent to which the parent institution (sponsor) benefited from the program. Here your focus shifts from the relative benefit to the client, to the relative benefit to the sponsor. Was the expenditure of resources worth it for the sponsor compared with what they realized in return (efficiency)? Did the productivity of a certain group of employees increase (effectiveness)? Did the program change the performance, the product, or the image of the sponsor (impact)? These are the macro concerns that this level of evaluation addresses so that decision makers conclude what programs really do to help their parent institution.

Formal Reasons to Evaluate

To know what type of evaluation to use, managers first set out their reasons for undertaking evaluation. In the public sector, for example, federally or state-sponsored programs demand third-party or internal evaluations; hence, the reason for these evaluations is that they are mandated. The mandate (the reasons for the evaluation) may be for fiscal purposes (that is, receiving the second year's funding may be based on the results of the evaluation) or for comparison purposes (that is, determining which method among several would be the most effective to continue funding).

Certain questions need to be addressed in a formally mandated evaluation. Questions of efficiency might be: When did you do the program or project? How much did it cost? How long did it take? Questions of effectiveness might be: What did you do? How well did you do it? What were the outcomes? Questions of impact might be: Did the program influence lives? Did the program add value? Table 1.1 shows sample questions for an evaluation of a project to develop an affirmative action plan.

Another formal reason for evaluating is to justify a program. For example, a superior may want you to evaluate or you may do it for yourself. Often teachers learn about new ideas at conferences, through reading, or from talking to colleagues. However, they feel tentative about trying out the new ideas because they are under the scrutiny of administrators, parents, and other teachers. A person who is committed to a process that has merit will evaluate the process so that support can be communicated in the presence of data. Gut feelings, perceptions, innuendo, and anecdotes are comforting, but they are not convincing to the people who require more objective evidence. Even data are not always effective in convincing people, but data at least act as a common currency to demonstrate the value of your case.

Good managers routinely collect data about their programs or projects in anticipation of the need to justify. Good questions to ask are the following: How does this program compare to similar efforts? What would I have done if not this program? Are the goals or objectives justifiable as viewed by clients, staff, or funding source? Did we accomplish what we set out to do?

The final reason for evaluating is to improve or change a program. In this case, you collect data to show to people who will make decisions about changing or improving a program. Questions to

TABLE 1.1 Questions of Efficiency, Effectiveness, and Impact (Affirmative Action Example).

Levels	Resources (manager working on the project)	Activities (obtaining commitment of representatives to serve on task force)	Strategy (task force of employees to develop plan)	Objective (affirmative action plan with support of employee advocate groups)
Efficiency	Cost per person contacted vs. planned cost?	Cost per group endorsing plan?	Cost of group-developed plan vs. manager-developed plan sent to groups for comment?	Cost per group actually supporting plan vs. planned cost?
Effectiveness	Was the selection of this manager the correct selection?	Diversity of the groups compared to diversity of the company?	Number of groups endorsing the plan?	How many groups actually adopt the plan?
Impact	Staff hours expended on this project vs. another project?	Has this generated interest from employees in sharing new ideas?	Has this approach been used in solving other problems?	Have the number of grievances filed been reduced?

answer are these: How will I use the evaluation in the program planning process? Is it meant, for example, to upgrade or change program personnel or to ensure accountability for expenditures?

Evaluation may also be performed in anticipation of seeking funding from either internal or external sources. A good example is the teacher who learned at a recent conference about a new technique of computer conferencing as a method to improve writing skills. Knowing that it was highly unlikely that the school had the resources to equip her classroom with sufficient technology, she brought her own computer from home and allowed the students to experiment with conferencing in their writing assignments. The data collected from this activity were then used to support her efforts to obtain funds from the school system or some other external funding source for the purchase of the required technology. Granted, this evaluation effort will do little for the current learners. The data collected from them, however, will benefit future learners in that teacher's classroom. This evaluation's most useful contribution is to the program planning process.

Practical Application

When XYZ Corporation, whose goal as mentioned previously is to have a sales representative meet face-to-face with every client annually, decides to train its sales department, executives will want to look at how evaluation fits into the company's overall sales program. That requires taking a look at more than the current training program for sales personnel. XYZ will need to identify the standards by which training can be evaluated, evaluate its training and other possible programs, and then make decisions on the benefit to the company.

Think of the process in this simplified way: A company that places a high value on customer service will want to be sure its sales force sees clients face-to-face. Now the company wants to use its contact records and tracking program to plan the training program. Program planning will ensue and will include the criteria, goals, and objectives that allow for evaluation during and following training.

XYZ knows from its simple tracking program the number of times customers are seen and who among the staff are seeing them. It also knows how much of its product is sold each year so planners can build in benchmarks, the criteria of success that will guide their evaluation process.

Because evaluation means looking at change, evaluation shows up in every stage of the program. Monitoring begins as soon as XYZ chooses a training program. Have all possible trainees been recruited? Do these trainees have the prerequisite skills to succeed in the training? Do the trainers have the necessary knowledge and skill level to train? Ongoing evaluation at this point allows for midcourse corrections and can make a huge difference in the success of the program. (Chapter Three discusses monitoring in detail.)

Finally, evaluation is done after the program or project concludes. The evaluator looks only at final data. What happened to the trainees? Did the program do what it set out to do? This, of course, brings you full circle to your philosophy. In XYZ Corporation's case, what is happening to the sales force? Are they meeting their goal of seeing each customer more frequently? You, the evaluator, can clearly see the final outcome with an evaluation at the end of a program cycle.

Formative and Summative Evaluations

Evaluations that focus on examining and changing processes as they are happening are called formative evaluations; those that focus on reporting what occurred at the end of the program cycle are called summative evaluations. These concepts are amplified in Chapter Three.

Putting It All Together

When you define evaluation, you can think in terms of cycles. Consider XYZ Corporation's sales training program and how its circumstances pass through the cycles of goals → needs analysis →

program planning → implementation → formative or summative evaluation.

Program Cycles

Goals	Fulfill XYZ Corporation's mission: Serve internal customers by providing training that helps them develop sales skills and a highly motivated commitment to customer satisfaction. Serve external customers by understanding and providing for their needs (both stated and inferred).
Needs analysis	Identify needs, for example, the sales force's need for an introduction to the concepts of a high-performance work environment, customer satisfaction, and continuous improvement.
Program planning	Select a sales training program that addresses the needs. Decide on evaluation criteria: How will we know we have succeeded? Do we have measures already in place or do we need to develop or identify new ones?
Implementation	The program begins, but it is still fluid; are we reaching those salespeople who need the training? Changes can still be made.
Formative or summative evaluation	Formative, because ongoing feedback can allow the trainers to correct any problems.

The person charged with performing a program evaluation will find it helpful to think of evaluation in terms of a format. You should conduct an evaluation with the evaluation design format in mind, allowing it to guide you through the steps to a conclusion. Use the format in Exhibit 1.1. It is based on information you have already

EXHIBIT 1.1 Evaluation Design Format.

Project _____
Focus (formative, summative, or both)

Evaluation Question	Activities to Observe	Data Source	Population Sample	Data Collection Design	Responsibility	Data Analysis	Audience

acquired in this chapter and can be used to plan and conduct any program or project evaluation.

Strategically, your work on developing the format should begin at the last section of the exhibit: audience. Your first task—not your last—is to ask who is interested in the results of this evaluation. The term is placed last on the chart because it is to the audience—the funding source, the management, the team facilitator, or other audience—that an evaluator delivers the evaluation report. Determining the audience, or stakeholders, is an essential step. Not only does this help an evaluator focus the evaluation activities but it also gives an early view of how the results of the evaluation might, or might not, be used.

In XYZ Corporation the audience for the evaluation might be the sales team facilitator, who needs to know how the team members are progressing toward the team's goals. However, the audience might also be the XYZ human resource director, who wishes information on the effectiveness of the newest customer service training. Or the audience might be the XYZ plant manager, who needs to consider the impact the sales force has had on the marketing of the latest product line. Given these three examples, the evaluator might (1) focus the report on suggestions for program improvement as the teams are meeting, or (2) include knowledge gains from pretesting to posttesting, or (3) track and link six-month changes in sales to training. Each of these possibilities suggests different evaluation questions, data sources, subjects, data collection strategies, data analysis techniques, and interpretations.

These are the essential parts of the design format:

Evaluation questions are those that your audience needs to have answered in order to make cogent decisions. Examples of evaluation questions might be these: Did those who participated in the first quarter training program perform significantly better in the second quarter than those who did not? Did team leaders evaluate trainees' time management skills as being satisfactory? Did the overall number of face-to-face meetings with customers increase over the three-month period? These decisions might come during the program cycle (for a formative evaluation) or at the end of the program cycle (for a summative evaluation).

Activities are those program activities that will result in accomplishing the program objectives. The objectives may already exist as statements used to communicate to staff, clients, sponsors, and the powers-that-be the intended outcomes (accomplishments) of the program. Examples: To help the sales force recognize cues to customer satisfaction or dissatisfaction, to teach the sales force how to apply available technology to time management, to teach the sales force to turn face-to-face meetings into sales.

Whether or not the objectives have been stated, the desired activities still need to be stipulated so that the evaluator can make at least some causal connections between what the program did and what resulted. For example, trainees attend sessions in which they are taught how to use the company's available technology to enhance their time management skills. The sales force meets with the trainer to discuss customer cues and to role-play responses to those cues.

Data sources can be both existing records the evaluator can examine for data, and the instruments that will be used to collect new data. At XYZ Corporation, the sales records prior to training and after training could become data sources. Others include individual achievement records of the sales force before and after training. Attitude surveys might be administered to internal customers (the sales force) as well as to external customers. Pretests and posttests may be administered to measure growth in time management and technology concepts and skills.

Population sample identifies those individuals from whom or about whom the data will be collected. In the case of XYZ, the individuals from whom or about whom the data will be collected are the sales force as well as their customers. There are 18 people in the sales force sample and 162 customers in the external sample.

Data collection design illustrates the context and schedule for the data collection. At XYZ, some data might be collected from pretests and posttests, that is, collected prior to the training initiative and following it. Data from existing records could be assembled before the training. Attitude scales would be administered to customers prior to the sales force training and again six months following the training.

Responsibility delineates who will have the responsibility to perform each evaluation activity.

Data analysis outlines how the evaluator will analyze and interpret the data after collection.

Questions and Exercises

Now that you have read Chapter One, return to the questions that you were asked to keep in mind at the beginning of the chapter.

1. What do all evaluations have in common?
2. How would you characterize the differences in the efficiency, effectiveness, and impact of a program?
3. Why evaluate in the first place?

Answer those questions in two ways:

- Write a general answer that applies to the chapter material.
- Use your new understanding to write a specific answer that applies to Scenario One. Be sure to address these issues:

   Should the program or project be evaluated?

   What level of evaluation— efficiency, effectiveness, or impact— do you think would be appropriate?

   What philosophy of evaluation applies?

Exercise I

Everyone has projects in which they are involved. Think about one such project. It could be something at work such as a new training program, or something in the community such as the latest fundraising effort for the local YMCA, or something in your personal life such as planning for the purchase of a new automobile. Now begin thinking about how you might evaluate that effort. Do the following:

1. Briefly describe the project (purpose, goals, activities that will be performed, expected outcomes).

2. Tell why you would want to evaluate it.

3. Reread the statements (page 4) that reflect two different philosophies of evaluation. To which do you subscribe? Explain why.

Exercise II

Recall that an evaluation is guided by your reason(s) for doing the evaluation in the first place. Therefore, you need to determine whether you want to assess the efficiency, the effectiveness, or the impact of the program. For each of the following four scenarios, determine the evaluator's reason (efficiency, effectiveness, or impact) for the described evaluation scenario, and then justify your choice.

1. A navy hospital's program to train nurses to work with terminally ill patients is in its second year. An evaluation will be conducted to find out whether the participating nurses have access to the texts and audiovisual materials they need and if they are actually counseling patients. This information will be used to examine the use of resources.

Context: _____ Efficiency   _____ Effectiveness   _____ Impact

Justification:

2. One of the northeastern states has commissioned an evaluation to measure the attainment of its capital management goals. Based on the evaluation's findings, the state may launch a personnel search.

Context: _____ Efficiency   _____ Effectiveness   _____ Impact

Justification:

3. The federal Department of Health is conducting an evaluation of its ten-year-old blood donor program. The evaluation will produce information about the number and characteristics of people involved in the program and the nature of the communities being served. The evaluation information will be used to determine if modifications in the program are needed, and if so, where.

Context: _____ Efficiency   _____ Effectiveness   _____ Impact

Justification:

4. The University of Rhode Island has begun a program to stimulate research about how adults learn. The foundation that sponsors the program requires an evaluation at the end of the first year to be used as a basis for deciding whether to fund the program again.

Context: _____ Efficiency   _____ Effectiveness   _____ Impact

Justification:

(Answers: 1–efficiency; 2–effectiveness; 3–effectiveness; 4–impact)

2

Why Evaluate?

SCENARIO 2   Ruth had never written a grant application. With guidance from the staff, however, she volunteered to help in the process. The grant required statements of the organization's mission, as well as statements of the goals of the gardening program, the activities involved, staff involvement, the cost of the program for the first and succeeding year, and the evaluation plan that would be put into place.

Ruth was not alone in having little experience in writing grants. The Proposal Development Committee felt that they, too, would not be able to answer all the questions posed by the grant application. They fully expected to have to call the Cox Foundation themselves for further explanations on a number of points. One thing that everyone knew, however, was that the application asked how they planned to evaluate the program. Only a few staff had ever been involved in a full-fledged evaluation. Also, not all the staff members were familiar with foundation grants, so they, too, would learn some new skills. At their first meeting, they wondered aloud how they might "prove" that the gardening program had been a worthwhile undertaking for the residents—as well as being worth the $2,000 it would cost to get started.

Neither Ruth nor the committee knew the term "learning moment," but it most certainly applied to them at this time

(Gray, 1998). Certainly, both the staff and their volunteer, Ruth, saw potential for the organization to learn through evaluating the gardening program. Although they were not yet in a position to delineate the learning that would take place, they were beginning to talk about why they would do the evaluation. Was it simply because the Cox Foundation mandated it? Who else at the retirement facility—staff, management, clients—might be interested in the results? What would be the benefits and limitations of evaluation? Was this organization, while seemingly cohesive and working in a climate of trust, risking anything by examining failures as well as successes (Gray, 1998)? Finally, Ruth wondered to what extent the evaluation would change her program.

The topics in this chapter address many of the questions and concerns surfacing at this stage of the evaluation planning process at Grandview Retirement and Nursing Facility. Think about the following questions as you read this chapter:

1. What are the benefits and limitations of an evaluation?

2. What factors ensure that an evaluation will be successful?

3. How might one use evaluation results?

When you finish reading, you should be able to answer the questions as they relate to the preceding scenario, as well as to the chapter material.

Key Words and Concepts

Resources: The total means or assets—time, people, funds, space, and so on—available for a program or project

Stakeholders: Organizations and people who are involved in or affected by the performance and results of a program or project

Standards: Agreed-upon measures of comparison in a program or project

Benefits

As the Preface stated, where there is a program, there should be evaluation. Answers to the "Why?" in this chapter's title emanate from different vantage points: management may ask for it; planning and policymaking may require it; or researchers interested in testing a principle or thesis may demand it. More on each of these requirements follows.

Benefits to Sponsors and Staff

But first, let's consider the "why" that emanates from the potential benefits to be derived. Regardless of whether a program is funded with public (tax) funds or private (foundation, company, or individual) funds, at some point those dispensers of the funds will probably ask, "What did we get for the money?" The results of evaluation activities provide you with some data to back up your inklings about the relative value of the activities, the effectiveness of the processes, and their impact on the people involved and the organization. Additionally, when staff members engage in evaluation, they find themselves talking to each other. Even conversations that center on evaluation procedures can act as a staging ground for good professional discussion on the program and its processes. Thus, an outgrowth of such communication is staff's appreciation of each other's ideas and of each other as colleagues.

The staff benefits in other ways as well. They need to know the definitions, potentials, and limitations of evaluation. Formal evaluation helps them select and state appropriate standards, indicators, evidence, and resources. This requires some level of scrutiny of a program from the perspective of the evaluation's philosophy, its procedures, and its anticipated outcomes. Staff members learn from this process, the program is improved as a result of this learning, and the client, eventually, is the beneficiary. Evaluation can also help staff to build a greater advocacy for their particular position. Caution is urged here, however, so that evaluation does not appear to be self-serving, a whitewash that points out only positive aspects. Evaluation should also point out program weaknesses, if any are found.

Opportunities

The evaluation might also present an opportunity to identify new audiences and applications for a program. An evaluation with good follow-up not only provides diagnostic data about participants in one particular intervention but also uses this diagnosis to improve subsequent learning activities for other participants. Through evaluation we can look at different ways to approach a task, different audiences the approach might benefit, and additional needs of the current audience.

Understanding of Outcomes

In the end, the benefits of evaluation include an increased knowledge of outcomes. Outcomes are what occur as a direct result of an action (that is, training, services, and teaching), usually measured immediately after an activity has been performed. The purpose of such an evaluation is to determine whether the action was effective in doing what it set out to do. Sometimes the outcomes are those that were anticipated and sometimes they are surprises. These surprises might be of a positive or negative nature. For instance, a training program might be designed to prepare line workers to become supervisors. An anticipated outcome would be that the line worker obtains the information needed to function as a supervisor of other employees. An unanticipated outcome might be the "weeding out" of individuals who now realize that the role of supervisor is not something they want or can do.

Longer range, more sustained results of an action may be termed "impacts," which need to be measured after a period to allow for things to percolate and settle in. For example, a training session may be deemed effective, given the impressive outcomes after its completion. However, within three months, due to lack of retention or lack of use or "buy-in," the new knowledge has not been put to use in the workplace. Thus there was little or no impact from the training.

Impact is an especially important factor when the action is attempting to change behavior or attitudes. Individuals will often be able to tell you that they know something (cognitive), but whether they actually incorporate that new knowledge into how they think and perform might be a different matter.

The measurement of learner outcomes, community outcomes, employment outcomes, or employer satisfaction formulates the basis upon which people make decisions about the worth of programs. Of course, an essential part of the process is maintaining records of both intended and unintended outcomes.

Limitations

When we discuss the "Why?" of evaluation and the subsequent benefits, it may be tempting to ignore the opposing concept: evaluation has potential limitations. To begin with, evaluation does not guarantee change. There is always the possibility that the resources allocated to evaluation will not result in any improvement of the program. However, the fact that improvement cannot be guaranteed is never an excuse for canceling the evaluation.

Other limitations include the fact that formal evaluation will undoubtedly lead to wider disclosure of information to various audiences. When more is known about a program, it is open to more scrutiny and possibly criticism. This is especially threatening to the people involved in the program or projects who may fear having their shortcomings disclosed. They may, therefore, create artificial settings, by behaving differently during the evaluation or by providing inaccurate responses in data collection, resulting in a biased evaluation. Of course, this can lead to perpetuation of the status quo.

Another limitation may be a focus on trivia. That is, a formal evaluation may imply that a program's worth is no more than that which can be behaviorally stated and measured. So an evaluation of the workplace literacy program in a factory may discover that the employees are learning to read and communicate in English during the classes. However, on the factory floor they still communicate in their native languages and do not communicate with fellow workers who are unable to speak those languages. The processes are effective but have little or no impact within the work environment. Nevertheless, management decides to continue the program with the goal that some of these employees will eventually be bilingual and bicultural managers for this plant and possibly for future plants in their native countries.

Considerations

Because of the preceding benefits and limitations, the decision to evaluate should begin with the following considerations.

Social and Political Situations

Successful evaluation depends on the political and social atmosphere that exists both internally and externally to the program. Who wants the evaluation? Who will use the evaluation results? Who will conduct the evaluation activities? To whom does the evaluator report? These are important questions to ask at the start of the evaluation so that all stakeholders involved (staff, director, sponsors, clients, and the evaluator) know the answers.

Successful evaluation depends on the skill with which the evaluation is undertaken. Credibility of the evaluation findings is directly linked to the credibility of the evaluator. The credibility of the evaluator is directly linked to his or her objectivity (being either a third party or recognized as taking an objective viewpoint), exper-tise, and experience with other evaluations. Even if the evaluation is designed well and executed well, if the report is carelessly done, the evaluation questions are not answered, the recommendations are not carefully thought through, or the data are inappropriate or unexplained, the results will not be accepted or used.

Successful evaluation depends on the ability and willingness of evaluation consumers to use and accept the findings. If, as men-tioned previously, the evaluation is not perceived as credible, the people needing the information will not use it. If the evaluation is presented as something that has to be done for funding purposes, then the evaluation results will be seen as something being sent on to the "powers that be" and will not be used. On the other hand, involvement of the consumers during the formation of the evalua-tion design and their input into the evaluation questions will help ensure that the results will be used.

Business organizations, communities, individuals, and agencies all have the need to evaluate, but they are compelled by different rea-sons. Some are compelled by management or administration to do so. Management or administration may be thinking of making shifts or changes, may change its vision of the organization, or may decide to take a different direction. Thus, the evaluation results may provide insights into the appropriateness of changing the mission, direction, or focus of an agency. The results may help improve service delivery by testing out new techniques, or comparing different techniques to find the most effective ones (Rossi and Freeman, 1993).

Anyone who has ever administered a program or project wishes it to succeed. Today's administrators and policymakers must do more than wishful thinking because the costs and accountability simply prohibit guesswork. Most funding comes with stringent re-quirements for reporting and accountability. Management looks for hard data for what the program does well and what requires change. Federal, state, and local governments, as well as corporate and agency boards, want to know whether specified standards have been met. Evaluation results become an integral part of complex decision making. Evaluation enables accountability.

Administrators may also see a need to improve the delivery of current programs or interventions. The impetus for an evaluation may be to compare a program or intervention to similar ones in other settings or similar ones in the same setting. A corporation, for example, might compare what it is doing to industry standards. Many companies will welcome the grueling evaluation processes of the Baldrige Award procedure simply to discover how they stack up against the industry standards. These findings may be used as baseline information for future planning efforts, or they may be used to compare their efforts with the competition, or they may simply be used as an ego boost.

Decision-Making Needs

A second answer to the "Why?" of evaluation is detailed in an organization's need for planning and policymaking. Evaluations are carried out to decide on the expansion or curtailment of programs, products, or activities. Using evaluation results, management may decide to advocate on behalf of their best-working programs, or to get rid of ineffective programs.

For example, an evaluation was conducted of a school-to-career program in a high school. The school schedules students out of academic classrooms and into integrated classes that have both academic and career or technical instructors and that can place students on-site in a variety of job locations for structured internships. The program was evaluated using the academic grades of students at the close of the school year, and the school-to-career students scored no better than the "traditional" students did.

The fact remains, however, that the school-to-career students spent less seat time in the classroom than the traditional students and some time in the community exploring the work world, but still had equivalent academic scores. When the students were followed for three years and found to be successful in the workplace, the program was deemed a resounding success.

This might be the kind of information that administrators need to change policies and procedures that have been in place for many years for no better reason than the fact that they have been in place for many years. In such a case the results of an evaluation of efficiency, effectiveness, or impact or some combination may be used to help make the decision to keep the old approach or change to the new approach.

Research for New Solutions

The third answer to the "Why?" of evaluation is for research purposes: to try something you think will work. You may try more than one approach and then compare the effectiveness of the two. This strategy may be used in agencies that wish to try a new, revolutionary, or miracle technique to solve a previously unsolved problem. More researchlike evaluations may be used when a company wishes to test new client groups or new markets with current procedures or products where there is no previous track record.

Perhaps you have surmised that the more there is at stake with the decision, the more "hard data" you might need to produce. Sometimes the gravity of the decision determines how extensive the efficiency, effectiveness, and impact of evaluation needs to be.

Putting It All Together

Any number of reasons propel a decision to evaluate a program. The decision to evaluate will change based on the level at which the resulting decisions (to fund, to keep or end the program, to select a different program) are to be made. Sponsors, or the people who furnish the resources to conduct the program, have a need for information from the evaluation, such as whether to continue providing the resources to program A, shift them to program B, or expand the program to new clients. Program staff, which includes the program director, other administrators, and the professionals who actually deliver the product, have information needs that probably focus on more immediate aspects of program operation. Community members, including the direct clients of the product, need to know, for example, what impact that program might have on their lives and their community.

Questions and Exercise

Now that you have read Chapter Two, return to the questions that you were asked to keep in mind at the beginning of the chapter.

1. What are the benefits and limitations of an evaluation?
2. What factors ensure that an evaluation will be successful?
3. How might one use evaluation results?

Answer those questions in two ways:

- Write a general answer that applies to the chapter material.
- Use your new understanding to write a specific answer that applies to Scenario Two. Be sure to address these issues:

  Should the gardening program be evaluated or should it not?

  What are some of the outcomes of the evaluation that you might anticipate?

Exercise

Look back to Exercise I at the end of Chapter One. You described an evaluation that you are either currently involved in or one that you want to initiate. Having read Chapter Two, you can answer these questions in reference to that evaluation:

1. Would the program you detailed in Chapter One benefit from an evaluation? How?

2. What are the inherent limitations in the evaluation of your program?

3. How might you use the results to benefit your organization, community, school, or yourself?

3

Decision Making: Whom to Involve, How, and Why?

SCENARIO 3   At Ruth's first meeting with Grandview personnel, she noted that the entire staff was not all in attendance, but there were representatives from each department—project coordinator, program staff, nursing, and administration. The administrator who had organized the meeting, Mike Ramirez, opened the proceedings and explained that although almost everyone would have a role to play in the gardening program, not all staff could attend each meeting during the work day, but each of the stakeholder groups would be represented. Someone would take notes and report to personnel who had not attended.

One staff member immediately asked whether a resident might be a logical addition as another stakeholder representative. After a brief discussion, the group decided to ask two residents to join them. This discussion started other staff members thinking about how the program would affect—if at all—the grounds crew and maintenance personnel. Again, the organizing committee realized that they needed to include another stakeholder group. These were, after all, people who would inherit a considerable amount of work. In addition, they would be able to contribute their knowledge of realistic costs gained from their steady ordering and maintenance of garden supplies.

Once the makeup of the committee was set, the group could begin to address the grant: mission, goals, staff involvement, activities, cost, and evaluation plan. At this point, a nursing staff person said, "Well, at least we don't have to worry about the evaluation question right now. That comes last." Luis, of program staff, answered that he wanted to suggest they look at the evaluation piece immediately. He had just been through the evaluation process with the program staff and the one thing they all agreed on was that they would never plan a program again without giving thought—early— to evaluation. It seems that when the administration asked just how effective their program had been, staff really had no substantive answer.

Now the committee wanted to know how the new program could be handled differently. Much discussion ensued, to the point that the meeting began to run long. Mike finally said, "What do you think about inviting an evaluation specialist from the university to advise us at our next meeting?" The committee quickly agreed and the meeting adjourned.

Think about the following questions as you read Chapter Three.

1. What is the connection between monitoring and evaluation?
2. How does evaluation fit into planning?
3. How can evaluation results be used in making decisions?

When you finish reading, you should be able to answer the questions as they relate to the scenario as well as to the chapter material.

Key Words and Concepts

Program planning cycle: The life of a program or project and all its related activities

Formative evaluation: An examination of a program or project in progress

Summative evaluation: Evaluation conducted at the end of a program or project for funders or for corporate or other decision makers

Monitoring: Assessing the extent to which a program is (1) undertaken consistently with its design or implementation plan and (2) directed at the appropriate target population (Rossi and Freeman, 1993)

Program and Project Cycles

Every program, no matter what its origin, has a life cycle through which evaluation activities flow. Everyone involved in the program, from those who fund it, to those who lead it, to those who receive its services or products, has a stake in the decision making. These are the people, the stakeholders, who need to be a part of the evaluation process. In a perfect world, the evaluator—whether internal or external—would be involved from the outset and would contribute to every phase of the life cycle, making sure that all the appropriate people were involved and receiving pertinent information along the way.

Overlooked Stakeholders

In the real world, unfortunately, some group or groups are left out. Sometimes the project staff members are left out because the evaluation is viewed as an activity being performed for someone else (that is, the sponsor), so there is no need to bother staff with more duties as they will not be recipients of the report. Usually the recipients (clients) are left out because "they don't really understand the program. After all, they are the clients."

Sometimes the evaluator is left out until the last minute because the project gets funded, the activities begin, and only then does the project director remember that an evaluation component was written into the proposal. Thus the evaluator begins work after the project activities have begun (in some cases when they are almost completed). Even an evaluator who is internal (one of the program or agency staff) is not necessarily included in (or attuned to) all phases of program planning.

Program Phases

To understand how, when, and why stakeholders are involved in an evaluation, you need to understand what evaluators call the program's life cycle. In one sense, the cycle of a program is unique to each and every program. In the public sector (education, human services, community-based organizations), the program cycle usually refers to the funding year, which is generally the fiscal year. Normally a program is funded for one fiscal year, so the evaluation looks at the program's progress over that period. Where funding is granted for two or three years, the evaluation may be able to examine long-term effects and the impact that the program might have had on the clients.

In the private sector (business and industry), program cycles may vary from several weeks to several years. The funding of the program may or may not come into play in defining the cycle. A decision maker may need the evaluation results of a two-week training program that introduces a new computer-based client data system immediately after each two-week session is completed, not after all employees have been trained. The information allows the manager to determine the extent to which the training activities are effective and the number of employees who need to repeat the training.

Because all programs and projects are different in purpose, size, time frame, and other factors, the evaluator must clarify the sponsor's mandate (Wholey, Hatry, and Newcomer, 1994).

The traditional program cycle starts with an organization's mission and goals, moves to needs analysis, through program planning (with the evaluation designed into the program plan), to program implementation where the formative and the summative evaluation take place. (See Figure 3.1.) During each of these phases, the evaluator can perform the functions that lead to evaluation findings, and ultimately to the evaluation report. At each phase, evaluation data can assist decision makers, bringing us right back to our main topic: Whom do you involve?

If the evaluator looks at the organization's mission and goals, decisions regarding the appropriateness of programs or program activities can be examined before the program begins. People do this every day when they are asked to make some hard decisions: Should the company be— can it afford to be or does it need to be— conducting certain activities? This scrutiny, however, is usually viewed as a fiscal process rather than a program evaluation process.

If the evaluator looks at the needs analysis, decisions about the actual need for or marketability of the program to the clients (internal or external) can be addressed before any resources are committed. Even though the "gut feeling" of some decision maker or even the "literature" seems to dictate that this is the program to pursue, the data collected from clients may convince you otherwise.

If the evaluator looks at the program planning processes, decisions can be made about the probability that the proposed activities

FIGURE 3.1 Program Cycle.

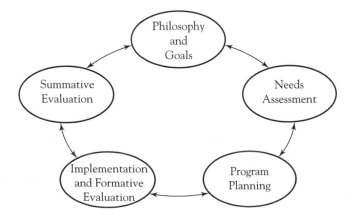

will indeed result in the needs being met. Furthermore, an efficiency evaluation at this juncture might help in making the decision to develop new activities rather than adopt or adapt someone else's similar activities. If for no other reason, involving an evaluator at this point will give the program staff help in formulating evaluation questions that will be meaningful to their conducting and improving the program. Also, the evaluation design can be created now and integrated into the overall program plan.

Usually it is in the program implementation phase that the evaluator is included in the process. The plan has been designed, ideally in response to real needs and in concert with the organization's mission, and now the evaluator is expected to collect data and, when the cycle is complete, make a report.

Table 3.1 later in this chapter outlines the information needs, the decisions to be made, and the contributions of an evaluator at the early stages of needs assessment and program planning and in the implementation stage when formative or summative evaluations may be conducted.

Evaluation and Monitoring

Often the process of monitoring and the process of evaluation are confused and even combined. However, the two processes are just that—two processes—because they are driven by different aims. Yet they have enough in common that each process can make some use of the other. When the requirement is to look at the extent to which a program is achieving objectives, you monitor what is being done and how it is being done. To carry out this task, you may use or create an evaluator's program description (EPD, discussed in Chapter Four). The EPD highlights a program's goals and objectives, the activities planned to accomplish the goals, and the measures you will use to evaluate the outcomes. Monitoring, in turn, provides some information that an evaluator can use to aid in decisions about improving, continuing, or discontinuing a program.

Monitoring includes activities such as continuous tracking of the flow of clients into the program, recruitment, intake procedures, and participation rates. Often an existing unit within the organization such as the accounting or management information systems (MIS) department performs these monitoring functions. If this is the case, the evaluator needs to discover what the department already collects and what the evaluator might have access to so as not to duplicate their efforts.

Monitoring efforts can also review the flow of services and activities that the program provides. Through the process of collecting data on attendance and retention in different activities, you will be able to determine early which activities are popular and which are not, which recruit but fail to retain, and which recruit and bring clients to completion. Such scrutiny can discover both the activities and the staff who need attention or praise. In your monitoring of activities, for example, you may observe lectures and look at how clients are progressing (learning). By observing the process of teaching and learning, you can begin to ask questions such as, "What milestones can I build into the evaluation design? Do the students have all the building blocks of the program so that they are prepared for the new learning?" This is where the evaluator enters the picture to collect evaluation data at the milestones as part of the formative evaluation. Thus monitoring functions support the evaluation, but cannot supplant it.

Finally, monitoring looks at the movement of clients: Are they returning for further learning? As a result of a training program, for example, have there been job changes? One of the key evaluation questions posed in most federally funded job-training programs is whether there has been a positive termination for the client. A positive termination is considered finding a job in the area for which the person was trained, or continuing with further training in the same or a similar area. Monitoring activities should collect information from clients and continue to collect these data even after the client has left the program.

These follow-up monitoring data can be used in the evaluation to determine program impact. Have you ever seen a recall notice on a product you have purchased? Now imagine receiving a recall notice for education or training you received. It could happen as a result of what was found in the monitoring data when it was examined in a formative sense. In other words, those employees who participated in the first two-week training on the computer system may need to be recalled if subsequent trainings were altered because of what evaluation results showed about what was learned or not learned in that first training.

The following example includes a list of sources that might be used in monitoring a job-training program. Although it is not an exhaustive list, it provides an idea of the methods and sources used to collect data and what could be useful to an evaluator.

Sample Data Sources for Monitoring a Job-Training Program

I. Visitation of job sites to assess the following areas:
    A. Compliance with the regulations, labor laws, and contract
        1. Nonprofit organization status
        2. Nonhazardous working conditions and duties
        3. Number of hours worked
    B. Supervision
        1. Adequacy (What is a supervisor's role in relation to enrollee? How much of working time is supervised? How meaningful is supervision? How are supervisor's evaluation forms utilized?)
        2. Handling of problems between an enrollee and a supervisor (How is it handled? How is it documented? Who is involved?)
    C. Enrollees
        1. Questions about or problems with job, supervisor, or counselor
        2. Verified age

D. Work habits: promptness, interoffice relationships, absenteeism; who instructs the enrollee regarding these habits?

II. Discussion with counselors to assess functions: intake; supportive services; certification, testing, and other evaluation; placement at job sites; counseling services; placement in unsubsidized employment where pertinent (and documentation of such); follow-up and documentation; documentation of all other functions; coordination among agency, community, job station, and other available services needed by enrollee

III. Discussions with other staff members (job developers, remedial education teachers, and others) where pertinent

IV. Reports: written summaries of all contacts with subgrantees, counselors, supervisors, enrollees, and others will be submitted to the director of the office and to the Department of Labor

The next list presents a sample of the types of data that might typically be requested and examined during one of many monitoring visits by either internal or external (that is, the sponsor's) monitors.

Sample Data Types for Monitoring a Job-Training Program

I. Contract compliance
   A. Simple review of contract
   B. Review of census information for the area serviced
   C. Review of invoices to date and comparison of actual monthly expenditures to what the average calculated monthly expenditures should be
   D. On-site review of contract specifications
      1. Enrollment figures, including client characteristics and residences, compared to contract figures
      2. Staff (interview) and facilities
      3. Outreach and recruitment
      4. Enrollee and staff files and time sheets and intake

     5. Quality of job stations and descriptions; supervisors' evaluations of enrollees
     6. Job development (including placement in unsubsidized employment)
     7. Termination or placement, exit interview, follow-up
     8. Employability plan for enrollees; quality and relevance of training to job market
     9. Assessment and orientation of staff, enrollees, and supervisors
    10. Services to clients: testing, counseling, transportation, and supportive services

II. Compliance with laws, regulations, guidelines
  A. Recruitment and processing of enrollees
  B. Enrollee eligibility (those deemed ineligible are checked also)
  C. Guidelines and regulations for economically disadvantaged people (unemployed, underemployed, or disadvantaged)
  D. Enrollee civil rights and affirmative action
    1. Signed statement
    2. Recruitment
    3. Placement
  E. Enrollee time and attendance records
  F. Review of waiting list and length of time for enrollees pending placement versus duration of employment possible for active enrollees
  G. Department of Labor laws (federal and state) with particular attention paid to the Fair Labor Standards Act of 1938
    1. Work permits
    2. W-4 or W-4E
    3. Safety conditions and working conditions

III. Exit interview: to discuss findings, obtain clarifications, feedback

IV. Reporting: findings (including documentation), corrective action necessary, follow-up visit to review implementation of corrective action

V. Availability of technical assistance: All staff are available at all times to subgrantees' clients who require or request assistance, information, and so forth. Monitors are constantly involved in technical assistance by virtue of the frequency of subgrantee visits and constant contact, either by phone or in person with program operators and staff.

As you can see, although some monitoring functions may be useful to an evaluator, much of the data they collect may be useful only to the monitors.

Program Planning Cycle and Evaluation

Just what kinds of roles does the evaluator play in the specific stages of program planning that were mentioned earlier?

Needs Analysis

In the needs assessment phase, ideally the evaluator is already involved and helping to identify the connection between program goals and the client needs that should be addressed. In a true needs analysis, a specific program has not been chosen yet. As the evaluator, your job would be to help clarify the goals, possibly to assist in identifying the needs, but definitely to help make the link between what the program sees as its mission (goals) and those identified needs. If a program were already in place, your help would be needed to look at the effectiveness of previous program activities vis-à-vis the mission.

Evaluation findings at this point are normally reported to people who allocate resources, for example, a funding agency. Anyone who has written a proposal for funding, either to a public or private source, understands that you need to clearly establish a link between the need for the funding and your capacity to carry out the proposed activities (to meet the need). The best way to do this is to describe what your organization has accomplished in the past (that is, previous evaluation results) and what you plan to do (or do differently) to address these new needs.

Program Planning

The second cycle in the life of a program or project is program or project planning. In this phase, high-priority goals have been identified. Now a method for achieving objectives must be selected. An important adjunct is planning the evaluation of the selected method(s). At this point, the evaluator can help program planners to develop, adapt, or select an evaluation design to meet their needs. In the case of the Grandview evaluation, the program director is one of the planners, and ultimately the evaluator, even though the roles are difficult to combine (Scriven, 1991).

For the program planner, this is the stage to decide on the specific activities to meet identified needs. These activities can be the same ones performed before (if they were effective), alterations of the old activities, or brand new ones. The program planner can, therefore, decide to develop new activities from scratch, adapt existing activities (from old or some similar program), or adopt some new activities, in toto, from a similar program.

During this program development stage, the evaluator helps to build the evaluation component into the program plan. As discussed earlier, if the evaluator is engaged during the planning of the activities, then the evaluation activities can be melded into the overall plan. Evaluation findings are normally reported to a variety of people, such as those responsible for instructional planning (for example, teachers, curriculum specialists, administrators), or community planning boards and human resource managers. Making the planners aware of what evaluation questions will be addressed, when, and how they will be reported, will help the planners see what feedback loops have been included in the plan. At this stage, the evaluation is typically included as an evaluation design within the program plan submitted to a funding agency.

Program Implementation and Formative Evaluation

As the program is implemented in the next phase of the program cycle, formative, or process, evaluation takes place. Process evaluation uses monitoring information or data. You are looking at performance, both the clients' progress toward attaining goals and the staff's effectiveness in performing activities. You are assessing the staff's ability to achieve its goals and objectives.

At this point, a program has been selected and put into operation. However, the program is still fluid so that modifications can be made. You may, in fact, be only halfway through a program when you critically assess whether it is on track—whether the activities are being effectively performed, and whether the activities are effectively meeting the need. Here the evaluator determines the extent to which the program is running as planned, measures the program's progress in attaining the stated goals, and provides recommendations for improvements. This involves, for example, pretests, interim diagnoses, or progress information on clients. As a matter of course, the evaluation findings in these reports (as well as monitoring data) can be used to end a program in midstream.

If the evaluation design does not include a formative component allowing for interim data to be used to alter program processes if necessary, but instead calls for waiting until the end of the program cycle for a summative evaluation to make these determinations, the program may have a serious problem. You, the evaluator, are trying to determine the interval of growth from point A to point B. The program's sponsor wants to know that money is being spent efficiently and for something effective. The formative evaluation allows you to change, or "tweak," the program where necessary. Then again, you may not be allowed to change the program if the funding source wants to see the results of the proposed program to compare it to another program.

Formative evaluation findings are usually reported to the program director and program staff, and are typically released throughout the course of the evaluation.

Also during this phase, monitoring may be going on. As described previously, monitoring is a data-gathering process that may have some or no connection to the evaluation. Process, or formative, evaluation can use monitoring data that directly relate to goal attainment. As noted previously, you are looking at the interval of growth from point A to point B during a program cycle.

Final Evaluation: Summative

In the final stage of an evaluation, called summative or product evaluation, the program has been running for some time. Procedures and methods are fairly stable and no changes will be made. The evaluator documents program processes, such as the number of learners who successfully completed the high school equivalency tests, and measures the attainment of specified goals. The summative evaluation also determines whether the program is experiencing any unplanned effects such as an increase in taxable income among people in a job-training program who were previously on welfare rolls but are now gainfully employed. Now the program can be compared to competing ones.

As opposed to formative evaluation, which examines a program in progress, the summative evaluation is an assessment of overall program effectiveness. This evaluation helps sponsors make decisions on future funding. Furthermore, the summative evaluation helps organizational decision makers decide whether to use the program again and whether to make it better in some way. Unlike formative evaluation, summative evaluation does not help staff to make adjustments during the current program cycle. In other words, summative evaluation does not interfere with the program and can, therefore, get a pure assessment of processes already in place.

The summative evaluation findings are released to people responsible for allocating resources and to groups concerned with program effectiveness only after the program is over.

Types of Evaluation for Decision Making

Use the planning schema in Table 3.1 to help you think about the program phase you are in and the evaluation functions that can or should take place.

Also notice in Table 3.1 how evaluation (both formative and summative) can assist in the decision-making process. At the least, the use of a structured evaluation in decision making will ensure that the decisions are data-based and much easier to support than "gut feelings."

Putting It All Together

Some people have a vision of evaluation and evaluators as engaging in a sterile process, a process led by people in white lab coats whose sole intention is to collect information that is going to get other people in trouble. If evaluation is performed properly, this vision could not be further from the truth. Granted, monitoring usually has at its core the collection of data on program functions that need to be reported to funding sources. Data collection for funding sources is aimed at helping them make decisions related to the overall impact of programs they fund and the continuing distribution of resources to those programs. Often, these monitoring data needs are viewed by program staff as not very useful to them, and probably quite intrusive. However, data collected as part of a monitoring function can be very useful in an evaluation. Both formative and summative evaluation processes should be designed to fulfill the information needs of the program staff. Ideally, the resulting data will assist program staff in improving program activities and policies.

Questions and Exercises

Now that you have read Chapter Three, return to the questions that you were asked to keep in mind at the beginning of the chapter.

TABLE 3.1 Program Planning Cycle and Evaluation Activities.

Decision to Be Made	Activity Description	Evaluation Findings Normally Reported to	Evaluation Findings Typically Released
NEEDS ASSESSMENT			
Identify high-priority goals that will serve as the basis for new or revised programs.	Select from among a full range of alternatives the goals to which resources should be committed. Determine extent to which current program is achieving the high-priority goals.	People responsible for allocating program resources (for example, funding agency; district, state, local administrators) People responsible for planning program and related activities	When the evaluation is completed
PROGRAM PLANNING			
Decide the means for achieving previously selected goals.	Select and develop the program most likely to attain goals. Include in the plan evaluation procedures for the proposed program.	People responsible for related planning (for example, teachers, curriculum specialists, administrators) Community	Evaluation plan within program plan submitted to funding agency

FORMATIVE EVALUATION			
Decide where improvements in an ongoing program are needed.	Measure program processes and components to ensure the program is following the plan. Assess achievement of program goals. Recommend improvements in program where needed.	Program director Program staff	Throughout the course of the evaluation
SUMMATIVE EVALUATION			
Determine the overall effectiveness of a fully developed program to aid in deciding whether to continue, expand, or drop the program.	Measure program outcomes and document program processes to permit informed decisions about overall effectiveness.	People responsible for allocating program resources Groups concerned with program effectiveness	When the evaluation is complete

1. What is the connection between monitoring and evaluation?
2. How does evaluation fit into planning?
3. How can evaluation results be used in making decisions?

Answer those questions in two ways:

- Write a general answer that applies to the chapter material.
- Use your new understanding to write a more specific answer that applies to the scenario. Be sure to address these issues:

  Apply the term "levels of evaluation" to the scenario.

  What will the foci of the evaluation be in terms of clients, staff, and administration?

  What are some of the decisions that might be addressed?

Exercise I

The Center for the Study of Evaluation has developed a four-stage evaluation framework:

1. Needs assessment
2. Program planning
3. Formative evaluation
4. Summative evaluation

During each of these stages, the people responsible for conducting an evaluation focus their attention on certain activities. In this exercise, you will be given a list of six situations calling for an evaluation. Your task is to select the evaluation stage that is most appropriate for the situation.

For each of statements one through six, decide which of the four types of evaluation activity would be most appropriate to the situation described.

Needs assessment = NA   Formative evaluation = F

Program planning = PP   Summative evaluation = S

1. In the last three years, school bond propositions for the Eagle-cliff District have failed in the polls. The school board conse-quently is faced with making budgetary cutbacks in the district's program. They decided to conduct an intensive eval-uation of three well-established instructional programs in order to decide what cutbacks to make.

   Evaluation activity: NA   PP   F   S

2. The Westchester School District will receive a considerable grant from funds established by the Emergency School Assistance Act if the district can supply clear justification for the manner in which the funds will be spent. The act states that "funds are to be allocated for a program only in cases where a consensus concerning high-priority in-structional objectives has been reached among parents and school staff."

   Evaluation activity: NA   PP   F   S

3. Normal High School has a large proportion of students who tend to drop out of school at the age of sixteen. Several semes-ters ago one teacher instituted a program in her homeroom with the aim of motivating students to remain in school until receiving their diploma. The program, which at first operated in an informal way and with few materials, has gradually developed into a systematic course of study that requires a great deal of teaching time. The school principal wants to know whether the program is worth the investment of time; if so, the principal would like to have the program administered in all homerooms. An evaluator from the school district has been called in to provide the principal with information about the program's effects.

   Evaluation activity: NA   PP   F   S

4. Last year, the state of Euphoria allocated several million dollars to school districts on the basis of district plans for administering new preschool and day-care programs. Most of the plans funded by the state were based on new research in child development and were, therefore, experimental in nature. A large-scale evaluation effort was consequently commissioned by the state legislature to monitor implementation of the plans and to periodically measure the children's progress in meeting prespecified objectives.

   Evaluation activity: NA   PP   F   S

5. Mount Olive Junior College recently installed a language laboratory with tape recorders, workbooks, and an extensive library of references. Though the language instructors are willing to change their usual method of teaching so that they can take advantage of the new equipment, they are not familiar with alternative methods of teaching language with adjunct materials. In addition, several instructors are worried that a change in instructional approach will have a negative effect on students' learning. A consultant has been called in to help make efficient use of the language laboratory and to suggest ways for measuring results of new instructional approaches.

   Evaluation activity: NA   PP   F   S

6. Bimonthly meetings of the staff of a new reading program at Lark Elementary School usually end up in controversy. Some teachers complain that the amount of record keeping for the program is so massive that they cannot keep track of student progress, and others are dissatisfied with the schedule. However, teachers with slow readers claim that the program guidelines are working splendidly. The principal decides to call in an evaluator to help solve the problems with the program.

   Evaluation activity: NA   PP   F   S

(Answers: 1–S; 2–NA; 3–S; 4–F; 5–PP; 6–F)

Exercise II

Once again, think about the evaluation activity you outlined for yourself at the end of Chapter One. Now look back to Table 3.1. Decide what type your evaluation falls into. Then go on to consider what major variables and major decisions are involved.

4

Starting Point: The Evaluator's Program Description

SCENARIO 4   Mike Ramirez called the new meeting to
order and introduced Judy Hallowell, who had come to help
the organizing committee address the issue of evaluation in
the grant proposal. The first thing Judy did was to congratu-
late the group on dealing with the evaluation component during the planning stage of the new program. "I understand that
you want to include a gardening program in your offerings."

"Yes," the program director said, "but we're interested in this
for reasons other than the beautiful flowers that Ruth grows."

"Oh?" Judy said. "What are the reasons?"

Mike told about their commitment to education and what
they had learned about the connection between mental and
physical activity and sustained good health and longevity.
Others on the staff filled her in with anecdotal evidence showing that this was apparently true for many of their residents.

Judy asked them if they had ever engaged in an evaluator's
program description. Because their answer was a universal
"No," she decided to begin immediately with an explanation
of that technique and then have the committee get started on
one while she was there. Judy started by noting that she had
come on very short notice, which she was happy to do, but she
had not had time to learn about the objectives of the gardening program, or even for whom they were doing the evalua-

tion. Judy said, "Can you tell me more about the purpose of the gardening program, the funding source you've found, and what you need to do to receive the grant?"

The committee answered Judy's questions and she continued to engage the group in discussion about their goals, the activities they proposed, how they would know whether or not their activities led to success, and what effects they expected might occur as a result of the program. About this time, Judy felt that the group was ready to make headway with the evaluator's program description (EPD).

Think about the following questions as you read Chapter Four.

1. What is the purpose of an EPD?
2. What are the components of an EPD?
3. How does an evaluator develop and use the EPD?

When you finish reading, you should be able to answer the questions as they relate to the preceding scenario as well as to the chapter material.

<hr>

Key Words and Concepts

Evaluator's program description (EPD): A statement prepared by the evaluator after working with stakeholders to amplify and clarify all aspects of the program including goals, objectives, activities, and anticipated outcomes

Evaluation questions: Questions that will be answered by the evaluation and are based on the EPD

What an Evaluator's Program Description Can Do

In this chapter, let us assume that the first three phases of the program cycle have been addressed; that is, you have identified program needs and have devised plans for addressing these (either brand new activities or altering what was already in place). See Figure 4.1.

A second assumption is that you have clearly stated standards. These standards can be those imposed on a program by a parent organization, provided to the program from the professional field, developed by the staff themselves, or some combination of these. The standards act as the yardstick against which program activities and outcomes are measured. The measurements, however, may be part of the monitoring function (for example, recruitment or retention rates) or part of the evaluation process (for example, change in behavior or learning gains).

When your intent is to look at the extent to which a program is leading to achieved objectives, you are monitoring a program's processes, looking at what is being done and how it is being done. This monitoring function can be facilitated with an evaluator's program description (EPD).

How does an EPD tell you what you want to know? First, it reveals a program's goals and objectives. Second, it allows you to know and record the activities that are planned to accomplish the goals and objectives. Finally, it reveals what measurement tools are in place. There may already be a document that tells what you need

FIGURE 4.1 Program Planning Cycle.

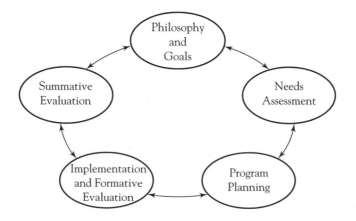

to know, serving the purpose of the EPD. Or you, the evaluator, may have to write that document after talking to staff and other stakeholders. In other words, you will amplify, clarify, and otherwise "do your homework" to make all aspects of the program clear.

In case you are wondering if the focus of every EPD is the same, the answer is emphatically no. You need to know with whom you are doing the EPD. Are you doing it with project staff? With the funding source? With the board of directors? As you ask questions and collect information, you will begin to understand that each of the preceding vantage points will result in a different EPD. The project staff may say that the main objectives of the program are to provide clients with job skills. The sponsor may feel that the main objective is to get people off the welfare rolls and onto the tax rolls. The board of directors may feel that the main objective of the program is to round out the offerings of the ACME Adult Learning Center and better serve the community. Perspectives on measurements may be as disparate as the goals. Probably the most agreement will come on the planned activities. Given these potentially different views of reality, the evaluator needs to clearly understand who will be the main recipient of the evaluation and gear the EPD for that group. If there will be multiple recipients, then there must be multiple EPDs.

The information you obtain from the EPD will assist you later in developing an evaluation design format. The EPD will help an evaluator to assist the funding recipient in formulating evaluation questions.

Developing an Evaluator's Program Description

How does an EPD get under way? The evaluator meets with all concerned parties. They may be staff, a board of directors, a program or project director, designers, engineers, sales staff, or even concerned clients. Remember that the EPD may be focused for any of these stakeholders. The evaluator begins by telling what he or she knows about the general purpose of the program. Very quickly, the stakeholders will begin to fill in the gaps and generally amplify the evaluator's understanding. Following is an invented dialogue that will show how this tends to play out. The scenario is a meeting between the evaluator, the program director, who has administrative responsibility for the Drug Education Program for pharmaceutical students, and the program coordinator, who is in charge of the day-to-day operation of the program activities.

Look for statements of goals, what activities are planned to reach the goals, and what evaluation procedures are built into the program. Notice, also, how the evaluator asks relevant and important questions that emphasize and bring to light what is important to the organization and the program (Gray, 1998, pp. 6–7).

AN EVALUATOR'S PROGRAM DESCRIPTION DIALOGUE

EVALUATOR: As we discussed, the purpose of this meeting is to devise an evaluator's program description. Let's begin with my telling you how I understand the general purpose of the program. . . .

PROGRAM DIRECTOR: Let me interrupt to inform you specifically about our objectives and activities. One of our major objectives is to have students observe the effects of a variety of drugs on the human body.

EVALUATOR: Why is this important?

PROGRAM COORDINATOR: Usually, pharmacy students learn about the effects of drugs from lectures, textbooks, and from observations of laboratory animals; they rarely are given an opportunity to see human reactions to drugs. We think this is an important part of a pharmacist's training because it makes students more aware of potentially dangerous drugs as well as what happens when certain drugs are taken in combination with other drugs.

EVALUATOR: I see. Making pharmacists more aware of effects of drugs is your goal, and observing drug reactions is an activity to achieve the goal.

PROGRAM COORDINATOR: Yes, and in addition to the observation of human subjects, another activity for this goal is having students attend lectures on the nature and treatment of frequently occurring medical problems, like hypertension.

EVALUATOR: At the end of the program, how will you know if the students have become more aware?

PROGRAM DIRECTOR: All pharmacy students take a test that requires them to name the likely reaction when one or more drugs are administered to patients with certain medical conditions. We will consider the program a success if students who participated in the program perform significantly better on the test than students who did not participate in the program.

EVALUATOR: What other goals does the program have?

PROGRAM COORDINATOR: Another major goal is to teach pharmacy students how to audit medical charts to assess the appropriateness of the medications. We do this first by teaching our students how to read medical charts, and second, by supervising them as they do chart audits in nursing homes.

EVALUATOR: How will you know whether or not students can perform these assessments?

PROGRAM DIRECTOR: When supervisors evaluate their students' performance, we'll know if they find them to be satisfactory.

EVALUATOR: How about the accuracy of the audit results?

PROGRAM DIRECTOR: The coordinator also suggested checking the audits, but I have faith that the supervisor's evaluation is sufficient evidence of program merit.

EVALUATOR: OK. Are there any other goals?

PROGRAM COORDINATOR: No.

EVALUATOR: When I received some of the program brochures, I noticed that the legislation that funds this program requires that you teach students about laws relating to informed consent and malpractice.

PROGRAM DIRECTOR: You're right. That's not one of our prime goals, but we do devote part of our instruction to it. Obviously, we would not be eligible for funding if we didn't, so we discuss the laws and the professional situations in which they apply.

PROGRAM COORDINATOR: We measure their understanding by asking students to cite laws and their provisions.

PROGRAM DIRECTOR: Also, we ask students to identify situations in which the law does or does not apply.

As the evaluator, you can look at the EPD process graphically. As you reread the dialogue, just recall the items you were asked to look for. Try to sift out goals, activities, and evidence of program merit. The goals are those accomplishments of the program that are anticipated by the program designers. These might be what clients would gain from the program or what might be gained by the organization within which the program operates, or by the more generalized community in which the organization exists. Now look at Table 4.1 for information drawn from the preceding dialogue.

What questions does this particular EPD answer? We can summarize them as follows.

Questions Based on the EPD

1. Did those who participated in the program perform significantly better on the test than those who did not?

2. Did supervisors evaluate students' drug audits as satisfactory?

3. Were students able to identify situations in which a law does or does not apply?

An evaluator will take this questioning phase one step further by asking some questions not specifically based on the EPD, but which are nonetheless applicable and valuable to the dialogue.

TABLE 4.1 EPD for the Pharmacy Training Program.

Part	Goals	Activities	Evidence of Program Merit
1	To make pharmacists more aware of drug effects	Pharmacy students observe human reactions to drugs. Students attend lectures in the nature and treatment of frequently occurring problems.	Students who participate in the program perform significantly better on the test than students who do not
2	To teach students how to conduct drug audits using medical charts	Students are taught how to read medical charts. Students conduct supervised chart audits in nursing homes.	Supervisors give students satisfactory evaluations.
3	To be knowledgeable about laws relating to informed consent and malpractice	Instructors conduct discussions of laws and the situations in which they apply.	Students are able to cite laws and their provisions. Students are able to identify situations in which a law does or does not apply.

Questions Not Specifically Based on the EPD

1. How do the goals, activities, and outcomes of this program compare with other clinical programs for pharmacists?
2. What will be the benefits of increasing the program funds by 10 percent?
3. How well was the program managed?

With the EPD clearly outlined, the evaluator can begin to identify monitoring and evaluation activities. However, much of what goes into the evaluation activities is dictated by the purpose of the evaluation. In Chapter Three we discussed the reasons for evaluation in terms of whether it is to fulfill some mandate, to identify what is happening in a program, or to determine if one process is more effective than another. Using the preliminary information you glean from the EPD and the purpose of the evaluation, you will select a specific evaluation model. These models are covered in the next chapter.

Putting It All Together

With any project, you have to start somewhere. The evaluator's program description is a great starting point for an evaluation. If you are not intimately familiar with the program you are about to evaluate, then you need to learn something about the processes that are planned or are already in process. Also, you can learn about program staff perspectives on the crucial elements of the program simply by asking questions to develop the EPD. What questions do others want answered? What other stakeholders may need to be considered (Quinones and Kirshstein, 1998)? In the case of the pharmacy program, you have already conferred with the program director and program coordinator. Some stakeholders that you may want to talk to include instructors, supervisors, students, state officials, and other health professionals.

An interesting side benefit of the EPD process is the rapport that you can begin to develop with the program staff. Reviewing goals, standards, and activities and asking the good questions that result in an effective evaluation will align the thinking and actions of all concerned. This brings to mind a quote attributed to Sir Josiah Stamp of the Inland Revenue Department (England) between 1896 and 1919: "The government are very keen on amassing statistics. They collect them, add them, raise them to the nth power, take the cube root and prepare wonderful diagrams. But you must never forget that every one of these figures comes in the first instance from the village watchman, who just puts down what he damn pleases." Unless a rapport, a trust, is built between the evaluator and the program staff, they may tell you anything (truth or falsehood) they please and you may never know the difference. Or they may tell you nothing, which is just as bad.

The EPD provides you with information that you can use to develop evaluation questions and the evaluation design format that will guide your actions from this point forward.

Questions and Exercises

Now that you have read Chapter Four, return to the questions that you were asked to keep in mind at the beginning of the chapter.

1. What is the purpose of an EPD?
2. What are the components of an EPD?
3. How does an evaluator develop and use the EPD?

Answer those questions in two ways:

- Write a general answer that applies to the chapter material.
- Use your new understanding to write an EPD dialogue for Grandview Retirement and Nursing Facility. Be sure to address these issues:

What are the program's goals and objectives?

What activities are planned to accomplish the goals and
objectives?

What evaluation measures will be built into the program?

Exercise I

Take another look at the evaluation design format introduced in
Chapter One, as shown in Exhibit 4.1. Using the Exhibit 4.1 format, you can now transfer information from this chapter to the
chart. The evaluation questions are supplied for you. Write in the
activities planned for the pharmacy students.

Exercise II

Once again, think back to your own project that you detailed in
Chapter One. What are your evaluation questions for that project?
What activities have you planned? Place your answers to those
questions in a chart like the one in Exhibit 4.2.

EXHIBIT 4.1 Evaluation Design Format.

Evaluation Question	Activities to Observe	Data Source	Population Sample	Data Collection Design	Responsibility	Data Analysis	Audience
1. Have pharmacists become more aware of drug effects?							
2. Do students know how to conduct drug audits using medical charts?							
3. Are students knowledgeable about laws relating to informed consent and malpractice?							

EXHIBIT 4.2 Evaluation Design Format.

Evaluation Question	Activities to Observe	Data Source	Population Sample	Data Collection Design	Responsibility	Data Analysis	Audience

5

Choosing an Evaluation Model

SCENARIO 5   At the end of their last meeting, Judy
Hallowell distributed information on choosing an evaluation
model, with specifics on why, how, and when each model
might be employed. Judy asked the committee to read and
consider the information before today's meeting so that they
would be able to get right into the task.

Now that the Grandview special committee had supplied
enough information and worked with Judy so that she could
write the evaluator's program description, they were ready to
move on with their work. With Judy's help they would choose
an evaluation model that would aid them in conceptualizing
the evaluation task. Judy commented on some of the more
commonly chosen models—the discrepancy, transaction,
goal-free, decision-making, and goal-based models—and
answered the group's questions about what they had read.
Then the committee set out to decide which one fit their
circumstances.

In order to involve everyone in the decision, Judy suggested that the committee of eighteen people break into
smaller working groups. That way everyone would have a
chance to contribute to the discussion. Each group would consider such things as whether any of the models was clearly
unsuitable based on what was already known about the

gardening program. Also, she asked which models might work and why, according to the definitions and clarifications in her handout. Judy proposed that each group choose a spokesperson, and when they returned to the full group, they would pool their thinking and decide on a model.

Now the committee formed smaller groups and began their work.

Think about the following questions as you read Chapter Five.

1. What are some of the more popular evaluation models?
2. What are the component parts of an evaluation format?
3. What are the basic differences between research and evaluation?

When you finish reading, you should be able to answer the questions as they relate to the preceding scenario as well as to the chapter material.

<hr>

Key Words and Concepts

Hypothesis: An assumption; something thought to be true; a tentative expectation

Quantitative: Focuses on numbers, measurements, inductive reasoning

Qualitative: Focuses on perception, understanding through verbal means; deductive reasoning

More Than One Way to Evaluate

As the committee at Grandview learned, choosing an evaluation model would help all the participants to conceptualize the evaluation task. They would discover, however, that there is a wide range of models from which to choose. Indeed, modern evaluation practice has developed extraordinarily complex and sophisticated approaches that are beyond the scope and skills of the average manager conducting an evaluation. But evaluators at any skill level need to have some basic understanding of commonly used models and the ability to choose a model that fits their evaluation needs.

All the models for evaluation differ from research strategies in that evaluation results are provided to the appropriate stakeholders for the purpose of program or project improvement. The purpose of research, in contrast, is to draw causal links between observed phenomena and to add to the knowledge base on those phenomena, and the audience is the professional field in general. Thus an evaluator should beware the common mistake of confusing research with evaluation and consider for any model whether its focus is research or evaluation.

This distinction bears further explanation. Research involves the scientific method, which controls variables such as behaviors in an attempt to explain and predict. It assumes that all variables can be controlled and that there are discoverable causes; it is an orderly process. Research leads toward the development of knowledge; its inquiries stretch the envelope. Furthermore, the research process takes place in a recognized and defined arena wherein a formal hypothesis leads to the development of a research design. Data are collected and analyzed, conclusions are drawn, and the hypothesis is either confirmed or rejected.

For example, a local hospital believes that patient education for cardiac patients will be more effective if it involves more than the "traditional" discussion and written materials after a cardiac episode. Instead, patients are provided with a support group made up of other cardiac patients who meet on a weekly basis at the hospital. Patients are randomly assigned to attend or not attend this support group meeting after they receive the "traditional" patient education. They are monitored for six months to determine if there are any changes in lifestyle (for example, eating habits, exercise, taking medications) between the two groups.

Here a hypothesis was developed that the support group in addition to the patient education would be more effective in changing patient behavior than the patient education alone. Subjects are identified, a treatment is delivered, and data are collected and analyzed. Using the data, researchers accept or reject the hypothesis. These findings will add to the knowledge base on patient education techniques, and a hospital that wants to design a new program or change its current patient program may use these findings. The value of research to a program is discussed further in Chapter Eight.

In contrast, when you evaluate you are trying to learn what is going on in a particular program for people who are interested in *that* program. You are not trying to expand knowledge (although this does occur because many evaluation reports are published). You do

1. Establish evaluation questions (use your EPD to do this).
2. Create an evaluation design.
3. Collect data.
4. Analyze data.
5. Draw conclusions from data.
6. Make decisions on a program's efficiency, effectiveness, and impact.
7. Report to stakeholders.

As you expand your understanding of evaluation and reach the point of choosing an evaluation model, you will want to understand the meaning of two other terms: qualitative and quantitative evaluation. Quantitative evaluation emphasizes facts that can be stated numerically, and qualitative evaluation emphasizes understanding through verbal narratives and observations rather than through numbers. (These terms are discussed in greater detail in Chapter Six.) Both quantitative and qualitative methodologies and data can be used in all the models. In the preceding example of the patient education program, if the data collected were observations of patient behavior, anecdotal accounts from the patients and family members, or responses to a survey that the patient completes, they might be considered qualitative in nature. If the data collected, however, were blood cholesterol levels, electrocardiogram readings at several points over the six months, or the patient's weight, they would be considered quantitative in nature.

Five Evaluation Models

Here are five models of evaluation that will help you conceptualize the task you have set out to do.

Discrepancy Evaluation Model

The discrepancy evaluation model, developed by Malcolm Provus (1971), is used in situations where there is an understanding that a program does not exist in a vacuum, but instead within a complex organizational structure. The model assumes that the aim is not to prove cause-and-effect relationships but to understand the evidence well enough to make reasonable assumptions about cause and effect. In other words, there is more interest in why something might have occurred rather than the fact that it did occur. A program is examined through its developmental stages with the understanding that each of the stages (which Provus defines as design, installation, process, product, and cost-benefit analysis) includes a set of standards of performance. The program developers had certain performance standards in mind for how the program should work and to identify whether it was working. This model helps you to make decisions based on the difference between preset standards and what actually exists.

The program cycle framework used for this model corresponds roughly with the program cycle framework presented in Chapter Three but focuses on points for discrepancy evaluation. The design stage here equates to the needs analysis and program planning stages; installation and process are parts of the implementation stage where formative evaluation is done; and the product and cost-benefit analysis stages equate to a summative evaluation stage.

Use of the discrepancy model begins with a meeting to work on an evaluator's program description. All levels of program staff are invited and the large group is divided into smaller, workable groups. These groups respond to questions developed by the evaluator to elicit their ideas on how their program is designed. The resulting description of the design is then compared to design standards (devised by the sponsor or drawn from standards for the field or from some other source). The discrepancies that are observed, if any, between the standards and the developed design are communicated back to the staff for review and action. Now the evaluator can use the assessed design in the installation (or implementation) stage as the standard with which to compare the program's operation. The evaluator looks—with standards in mind—at staff and at clients and how they move through the program. A discrepancy evaluator's role is to determine the differences between what is and what should be. Again, this information is communicated back to the staff for any midcourse corrections.

In the process stage, there is a comparison between what is being accomplished (by clients, staff, and others) and the interim products that were anticipated. Here the evaluator communicates the degree to which these interim products have or will be achieved. In the product stage, the evaluator compares the degree to which the end products (for example, student learning, behavior change, and increased productivity) are in line with what were identified as anticipated end products in the original design.

In the final stage—cost evaluation—the evaluator compares the cost of similar programs having the same or a similar end product. Using the conclusions from this stage (and perhaps from the product stage as well), sponsors can make a policy decision to continue or end the program. Usually, this final stage is referred to as return on investment or cost-benefit analysis.

The discrepancy model is useful to a program staff that is interested in and able to have an evaluator working with them from the outset of program operation. The strength of this model is in having the staff involved in determining and using the evaluation criteria and standards.

Goal-Free Model

In the goal-free evaluation model developed by Michael Scriven (Popham, 1974), the evaluation looks at a program's actual effect on identified needs. In other words, program goals are not the criteria on which the evaluation is based. Instead, the evaluation examines how and what the program is doing to address needs in the client population. With this model, you observe without a checklist, but record all data accurately and determine their importance and quality. Categories naturally emerge from your observations. This model of evaluation can use all forms of obtrusive methods (subject is aware of them—for example, tests) as well as unobtrusive ones (subject is not aware of them—for example, a hidden camera) to gather data. The evaluator has no preconceived notions regarding the outcome of the program (that is, goals). The staff should not contaminate the evaluator's method with goal statements. The evaluator is trying to form a description of the program, identify processes accurately, and determine their importance to the program. As the evaluator, you are gathering data on things that are actually happening and evaluating their importance in meeting the needs of the client population.

A good example of this model is the process followed by the Consumer's Union (producers of *Consumer's Report*) in which the manufacturer's intent for the product is irrelevant to the actual usefulness to the consumer.

The goal-free model is the most difficult to use, especially when the evaluator is part of the program or project; yet it is a popular method because it can be used within a program that has many different projects occurring simultaneously. In such a situation the same client population participates in a number of activities, and it is difficult to separate the results of two projects' activities. In fact, program results might come from the interactions between two or more projects' activities.

For example, an evaluator might be asked to evaluate the effectiveness of an adult basic education (ABE) project housed within the program of a local adult learning center (ALC). Also housed in that program are workplace literacy, welfare to work, and adult computer literacy projects. Clients of the adult learning center may partake in any or all of these programs. Thus it would be difficult if not impossible to isolate the results of just one project's activities. A goal-free evaluation would examine the overall results for the clients of the ALC program, which would be more meaningful than individual evaluations of each project.

The person who performs the goal-free evaluation of the ABE project may have no subject-matter expertise in the field of adult education. This is a topic of debate among many experts. Some say the evaluator should have expertise in the field being evaluated; others say no expertise is better (Rossi and Freeman, 1993). The issue, of course, is preconceived notions. Some scholars say that an evaluator who is not familiar with the nuances, ideologies, and standards of a particular professional area will presumably not be biased when observing and collecting data on the activities of a program in that area. They maintain, for example, that a person who is evaluating a program to train dental assistants should not be a person trained in the dental profession. But other scholars allege that a person not aware of the nuances, ideologies, and standards of the dental profession may miss a good deal of what is important to the evaluation. Both sides agree that the evaluator must attempt to be an unbiased observer and be adept at observation and capable of using multiple data collection methods (Wholey, Hatry, and Newcomer, 1994).

Once the data have been collected, the evaluator attempts to draw some conclusions about the impact of the program on addressing client needs. This information is then delivered to parties interested in the evaluation results. Again, the evaluator using this model makes a deliberate attempt not to know about program goals, written proposals, or brochures that exist. He or she simply studies the outcomes and reports on them.

The goal-free model works best for qualitative evaluation because the evaluator is looking at actual effects rather than anticipated effects for which quantitative tools have been designed.

Interestingly, Scriven suggests using two goal-free evaluators, each working independently. In this way, the evaluation does not rely solely on the observations and interpretations of one person.

Transaction Model

The transaction model developed by R. E. Stake in 1975 (Madaus, Scriven, and Stufflebeam, 1983) affords a concentration of activity between you, as both evaluator and participant, and the project staff. The main beneficiaries of an evaluation using this model are the clients and practitioners.

This model combines monitoring with process evaluation through a constant back-and-forth between evaluator and staff. The evaluator is an active participant, giving constant feedback. In effect, the evaluator is or acts as one of the project staff members.

The evaluator uses a variety of observational and interview techniques to obtain information from the program staff and clients. This model may have a goal-free or a goal-based orientation. Instead of trying to achieve objectivity as in the previous models, the evaluator uses subjectivity in the transaction model.

Using the previous example of the adult learning center, the transaction evaluator might be one of the teachers of the ABE project who is assigned to follow a group of clients through the other projects in an attempt to distinguish any measurable results coming from a single project. The evaluator is one of the staff of the ALC, participating in and providing project activities. The findings are shared with the staff of all the projects to improve both individual projects and the overall program.

Decision-Making Model

The decision-making model developed by Daniel Stufflebeam (Madaus, Scriven, and Stufflebeam, 1983) is employed to make decisions regarding the future use of the program. In this case, you are not as concerned with how the program is going presently. Instead you are concerned with its long-range effects, such as the number of cancer patients who survive in a five-year trial, or the number who survive from this program as compared to another program with a different approach. The focus is on decisions that need to be made in the future.

For example, an adult education program might have three different commercial packages for teaching people with a low literacy level to read English. In previous evaluations all three packages have proven effective in teaching reading; however, the sponsors of the program need to cut funds and a decision needs to be made to discontinue the use of one or more of the packages. This is a decision-based situation that requires focus not on the client, the staff, or the activity but on how best to cut operating expenses.

This model is wide open in the methodology you use to collect data. Both quantitative methods (such as tests and records) and qualitative methods (such as interviews, observations, and surveys) might be employed. This choice depends on what the sponsor wants to know in order to make the decision; it is a totally summative evaluation.

Goal-Based Model

The goal-based model, also called the objective attainment model, is the easiest to use and therefore the most often used. The evaluation may be based on stated objectives or goals found, for example, in a proposal, brochure, or other description of the program. This model is not concerned with ancillary items, variables, or occurrences that might be spin-off products of the program activities, just stated objectives. The wording of the objectives would usually identify the tests and standards for the evaluation. The evaluator is looking to measure specified outcome variables, using quantitative or qualitative methods. This model can become the most research-like, especially if you can convince the stakeholders to use a control or comparison group, as discussed in Chapter Eight.

Other Models

Other models to consider are the systems analysis model developed by Rivlin, the art criticism model developed by Eisner, and the adversary model developed by Owens (Madaus, Scriven, and Stufflebeam, 1983).

In the systems analysis model, the evaluator looks at the program in a systematic manner, studying the input, throughput, and output. Input is elements that come into the system—for example, clients, staff, facility, resources—as they are prior to encountering the program. Throughput consists of things that occur as the program operates—for example, activities, client performance, staff performance, resource availability, and the adequacy of resources such as money, people, and space. Output is the results of the program—for example, client change, staff effectiveness, adequacy of activities. The evaluator examines the program's efficiency in light of these categories. This model might be employed to determine whether a program is getting people into the program and out of the program in an efficient manner, as well as achieving its goals.

In the art criticism model, the evaluator is a qualified expert in the nuances of the program and becomes an expert judge of the program's operation. The effectiveness of the model relies heavily on the evaluator's ability to judge objectively. This model might be employed when a program wishes to have a critical review of its operation prior to applying for funding or accreditation of some sort. In the private sector, for example, this model could be used to prepare for accreditation by the International Organization for Standardization (ISO). In educational circles, likewise, the accreditation process could prompt the use of an expert judgment.

In the adversary model, the evaluator facilitates a jury that hears evidence from individuals (sometimes adversaries) on particular program aspects. The jury then uses multiple criteria to "judge" evidence and decide what is actually happening. This model can be used when there are different views of what is actually happening in a program. These might be differences among clients, staff, community members, or sponsors.

Choosing the Right Model

The logical question at this point is, "How do I know which model suits my particular situation and needs?" This question is answered by looking back at your answer to the original question, "Why evaluate this program?" If it was to meet some mandate of a funding source or management, you might want to employ the goal-based model. If it is to learn something about your program so that staff can improve service delivery, you might employ the systems analysis or goal-free models. If your intent is to critically examine certain aspects of your program for reduction or promotion, you might use the decision-making, art criticism, or transaction models. The adversary model would be used when the purpose of the evaluation is to settle differences of opinion between stakeholders.

Table 5.1 will help you to decide which model to use.

Evaluation Design Format

Now that you have chosen a model to use, you can return to the larger picture that we introduced at the end of Chapter One, the overall evaluation design format. This format introduces the components that may occur in any evaluation: evaluation questions, program objectives, activities observed, data sources, population samples, data collection design, responsibility, data analysis, and audience. Not all components appear in each of the models—for example, the program objectives component is not used in the goal-free model—but most are common to all.

TABLE 5.1 Choosing a Model.

Model	Intended Outcome	Evaluator's Tasks	Sample Evaluation Questions
Adversary	Resolution of differences of opinion	Facilitation	What are arguments for and against program components?
Art Criticism	Critical reflection, improved standards	Expert judgment	Would a professional approve of program activities?
Decision-Making	Effectiveness, impact, quality	Data collection, analysis, interpretation	Was the program effective? What aspects of the program were effective?
Discrepancy	Compliance with standards	Facilitation, monitoring, data collection, analysis, interpretation	How did the program perform compared to standards?
Goal-Based	Efficiency, effectiveness, impact	Data collection, analysis, interpretation	Did the clients change (grow, learn)?
Goal-Free	Usefulness, impact	Data collection, analysis, interpretation	What happened in the program?

TABLE 5.1 Choosing a Model, *continued.*

Model	Intended Outcome	Evaluator's Tasks	Sample Evaluation Questions
Systems Analysis	Efficiency, effectiveness	Monitoring, data collection, analysis, interpretation	Were the expected outcomes achieved? Were the expected effects achieved efficiently?
Transactional	Program understanding	Participation, data collection, analysis, interpretation	What does the program look like from different vantage points?

Evaluation questions are central to all the models and all evaluations. As described in Chapter Four, these are questions that the evaluator or program staff or both develop to ensure that the evaluation results will address meaningful questions and lead to program improvement or promotion. These are much larger questions than those presented by program objectives.

Program objectives may be added at this point. These are the statements of intent that the program developers created to communicate what would be accomplished if the plan were implemented. These statements are the evaluator's friend because, if stated correctly, they will contain what is to occur (activity), to whom (client), the expected outcome (criterion), and how you will know (measurement). With this information, the evaluator knows what the staff will perform, what results they expect, and how they will measure program performance.

Activities are those specific activities that program staff will conduct for clients. It is important for the evaluator to know the activities and to which objectives they relate in order to identify a cause-and-effect relationship.

Data source is the instrument for data collection and recording. Depending on whether you will be employing qualitative or quantitative methods, your data source may be surveys, interviews, observation protocols, tests, or calibrated measuring devices. Your data source may collect new data from clients or contain already existing data on clients.

Sample refers to the individuals from whom you will collect data, specifically to the proportion of individuals in a program who are anticipated to participate in the evaluation. The term *population* refers to all the individuals who might be eligible to participate, and the term *sample* refers to those whom you will target to participate.

Data collection design is the schedule on which you will collect data. Depending on the model you select and the purpose of your evaluation, you may need to collect data before the clients interact with your program (pre) and after they have partaken of your activities (post). On occasion, you might collect data while they are partaking (interim) so that you can monitor change. The data collection design also communicates whether only those partaking in the activity will be included in the data collection or whether you will select a group of individuals who will not partake in the activity (control or comparison group).

Responsibility refers to listing, as clearly as possible, what evaluation activities you will perform as the evaluator. Those evaluation activities that you will not perform need to be identified, along with who from the program staff will be responsible.

Data analysis explains what statistical manipulations (if any) will be performed on the data collected. Each data set from each data source will probably have its own data analysis procedure.

Audience is the group for whom the report is intended. In some cases, the audience may be different for different evaluation questions. Sponsors, for example, may be more interested in evaluation questions directed at program efficiency and impact, whereas program staff would be more interested in evaluation questions on program effectiveness.

For example, if your task is to help sponsors or administrators decide the future of the program, you may elect to use the decision-making model. This makes the focus of the evaluation summative; you're not interested in how it's going at the moment but rather in the end results or effects. You need to report the program's effects to those who authorized or pay for both the program and the evaluation. So you can certainly say that you know the audience who will be interested in the evaluation you are doing.

Other Considerations

The eight models discussed in this chapter are by no means the only evaluation models available to you. Others offer different structures, foci, methods, and so forth, and hybrid models contain aspects of two or more of the models.

In Chapter One, we presented two definitions of evaluation that are commonly accepted in the field:

- Evaluation is the systematic process of collecting and analyzing data in order to determine whether and to what degree objectives have been or arc being achieved.
- Evaluation is the systematic process of collecting and analyzing data in order to make a decision.

Just by examining these two definitions, you can begin to identify which evaluation models might best suit an evaluator who is operating within one of these philosophical frameworks. Yet circumstances might arise in a particular evaluation that would require you to use whatever works for both the program and you.

Putting It All Together

In this chapter, we have presented the "meat" of evaluations and evaluation methodology. The models discussed provide a variety of ways to look at a program that is either clearly designed or not so clearly designed. The range of models allows an evaluator to be rather dogmatic in assessing a program against a preconceived set of standards and objectives, or fairly free to evaluate a program's worth based on what it produces—not what it said it would produce.

Organizations and the programs and projects associated with them have an abundance of people besides the evaluator who are assets to an evaluation. Because they have first-hand knowledge of the program or project, their contribution to the selection of a model may be extremely valuable (Gray, 1998). The evaluator should choose the model only if those being evaluated desire that to happen. Often those involved with the program see evaluation as one of those highly technical or complicated functions in which they "should" have no say, but that view is incorrect. All stakeholders should be involved in the decisions surrounding an evaluation, with the evaluator acting as the facilitator of the evaluation.

Using the chosen model, you create the evaluation format, which outlines the components of the evaluation matrix. These parts tend to flow in a systematic order, but they all stem from the evaluation questions. These questions represent the real interests of the stakeholders—what they want to know about the program in order to improve it.

Questions and Exercise

Now that you have read Chapter Five, return to the questions that you were asked to keep in mind at the beginning of the chapter.

1. What are some of the more popular evaluation models?
2. What are the component parts of an evaluation format?

3. What are the basic differences between research and evaluation?

Answer those questions in two ways:

- Write a general answer that applies to the chapter material.
- Use your new understanding to write a specific answer that applies to the scenario, addressing these questions: Which model would you choose for the gardening program? Why?

Exercise

Look back to Exercise I in Chapter One in which you described a project of your own. Using what you have learned in this chapter about choosing an evaluation model, which model would you choose for your project? Explain your choice.

Further Reading

Isaac, S., and Michael, W. *Handbook in Research and Evaluation: A Collection of Principles, Methods, and Strategies.* San Diego, Calif.: Edits Publications, 1995.

Madaus, G., Scriven, M., and Stufflebeam, D. L. (eds.). *Evaluation Models: Viewpoints on Educational and Human Services Evaluation.* Boston: Kluwer-Nijhoff, 1983.

Weiss, C. W. *Evaluation: Methods for Assessing Program Effectiveness.* Englewood Cliffs: Prentice Hall, 1972.

6

Data Sources

SCENARIO 6   As she had promised, Judy Hallowell came to the next committee meeting to work on an important aspect of the gardening program evaluation and the grant. That is, she asked the staff to pose the following questions to themselves: "How will I know if the gardening program activities have effected a change in attitude, activity level, health, or overall well-being of our residents? How do I acquire this information? What are my data sources?"

Many of the staff were not accustomed to looking backward—to earlier records   and then looking forward to creating new records of data on activities and their results. Judy coached them through identifying the items that were already available, such as Grandview's sign-up sheets for other programs. These showed the number of people engaged in activities on a steady or intermittent basis, which Judy said would be useful later. Neither had they really used to advantage the intake information regarding interests, attitudes, and skills, gleaned when residents first moved into Grandview.

Before the meeting concluded, Judy asked the group to brainstorm the many new sources from which data might be gathered. The staff, now very much into the process, swiftly listed such items as checklists, interviews, and surveys. At that point, Judy distributed information on the topic and asked the group to think about what her information on data sources had to do with their new program and the evaluation process.

Think about the following questions as you read Chapter Six.

1. What are the differences between qualitative and quantitative?
2. What are the levels of data that you might encounter?
3. What are some instruments that you might use or develop?

When you finish reading, you should be able to answer the questions as they relate to the preceding scenario as well as to the chapter material.

Key Words and Concepts

Nominal data: Mutually exclusive categories of data
Ordinal data: Rank-ordered categories of data
Interval data: Ordinal data that also have equal intervals
Ratio data: Data that have an absolute zero point

Starting Point

At the point you are ready to identify data sources for your evaluation effort, you already

- Know who the audience is
- Have had meetings with stakeholders to decide on evaluation questions
- Have written program objectives in hand
- Have decided on the program activities you will observe

As the program or project evaluator, you have already learned how to identify what a program intends to accomplish and how the staff anticipate meeting those objectives. You have also learned how to use that information to structure evaluation questions that will assist the staff in learning how their program works and might be improved.

If you know what you need to measure, you will now need to identify the data sources that will support your evaluation (or how you measure). The first step is to once again look back to the EPD process during which you asked stakeholders what, if any, data sources they currently had in place to monitor or measure program outcomes. If they are appropriate, you may want to incorporate those existing data sources into your evaluation design. However, if none of those in place are appropriate, or if they are outdated, incomplete, or unavailable because of privacy or other issues (Wholey, Hatry, and Newcomer, 1994), you will have to devise one or more sources suited to your evaluation.

Qualitative and Quantitative Data Sources

Two essential terms were introduced briefly in an earlier chapter: qualitative and quantitative. These terms refer to techniques for collecting data as well as to the data themselves, a key point in understanding these concepts.

The *qualitative* technique requires close-up, detailed observation (Wholey, Hatry, and Newcomer, 1994). First-hand observations are made by evaluators and result in descriptions of what is occurring in a certain program at a certain moment. The observer, who may or may not be a participant in the program, is interested in the present, not in final results. The focus is on meaning through verbal narratives and observations rather than through numbers (McMillan, 1992). Consequently, qualitative data are collected using data sources that include such things as observations, interviews, surveys, case studies, and existing artifacts and documents.

Quantitative techniques are used to establish facts numerically, to predict, and to show causal relationships. Quantitative data are collected using data sources such as tests, counts, measures, and instruments.

Four Levels of Data

When evaluators set about the task of collecting data, they need some basic knowledge of what types of data exist, what meanings are attached to each type, and how to choose, gather and analyze types of data that fit the evaluation. In fact, there are four levels of data—nominal, ordinal, interval, and ratio—presenting differing degrees of meaning and complexity. To begin with, however, you should know that qualitative evaluation deals with nominal and ordinal data, whereas quantitative evaluation looks at interval and ratio data. This will become clearer as you read about each of the levels.

Nominal Data

Nominal data are based on one principle, and only one principle. They exist on one level of discourse such as gender, ethnicity, religion, nationality, or marital status. *Nominal* means "to name." For example, in searching an employee database for a report, one might gather data on the employees' gender (male or female), job classification (sales clerk, sales representative, other), and educational level (high school, technical school, college). All the employees will fall into one category or another—male or female, sales representative or sales clerk, and so forth. Because the categories are mutually exclusive, individuals can belong to only one of them (Gatewood and Feild, 1994). You can add more categories within the level, but each should be unique so that the data you collect can be easily pigeonholed into one of the categories. The important criterion that makes this nominal data and really separates it from the other levels is that no order or value is placed on the categories. Nor is any order assumed, such as having a response of married comes before single which comes before divorced. The order is interchangeable because the order is meaningless.

Ordinal Data

Ordinal data are also based on one principle or level of discourse, but they do convey a rank order. Scales are perfect examples of ordinal data in that they range from one extreme to another. Data collected on a scale of agreement (from strongly agree to strongly disagree) are ordinal data. The categories within the response set are strongly agree, agree, no opinion, disagree, strongly disagree. An order is implied in these data where one comes after another. If you were to mix up the order, it would not make sense. Other examples of ordinal data are high, medium, low; and A, B, C, D, E, F. The important criterion that makes this ordinal data and separates it from the next levels is that although there is an order, there is no assumption of equal distance between each category. Ordinal data only measures the order, not the degree of separation. For example, if Donna, a team leader, were asked to rank team members on leadership qualities, the results might look like this:

Team Member	Rank on Leadership
A. B. Mendez	2
B. L. Wendel	5
C. D. Mulhern	1
D. F. Schoenberg	3
E. R. Good	4

You know that Donna believes that C. D. Mulhern exhibits the best leadership skills on the team. But do you know the difference in the leadership abilities of Mulhern and Mendez, who ranked second? No. Neither can you assume that the value of the distance between 1 and 2 is equal to the value of the distance between 3 and 4 or 4 and 5.

Interval Data

Interval data, like ordinal data, possess the characteristic of rank order, but they also involve equal intervals. In interval data the distance between any two consecutive points on the scale is the same no matter where you go on the scale. For example, the distance between a score of 2 and 3 is equal to the distance between a score of 235 and 236. Most numerical scales are interval data. However, what distinguishes interval data from the final level is that there is no absolute zero in this scale. Without an absolute zero, you cannot assume the equality of the negative numbers with the positive numbers. The distances between the points (that is, 1 to 2 and −1 to −2) might be equal, but the value of −1 to 1 cannot be equated to a similar interval on the scale. Test scores are usually interval data with the assumption that the distance between scores of 70 and 80 is equal to the distance between the scores of 90 and 100.

Ratio Data

Ratio data possess all the characteristics of the earlier three, but also have an absolute zero point. Examples of ratio data are weight and height. For example, we can say that Max, who weighs 160 pounds, is twice as heavy as Kim, who weighs 80 pounds. We also know that a manufactured microchip that fails below −20 degrees Fahrenheit and above +20 degrees Fahrenheit has a capacity of 40 degrees.

Nature of Data Collection

Nominal and ordinal data are usually referred to as qualitative data, and interval and ratio data are referred to as quantitative data, as mentioned previously. The purpose of this distinction is more for data analysis (discussed in Chapter Seven) than anything else, but it also has implications for how the data are collected.

Recall that an important difference between qualitative and quantitative data is how you collect it. Evaluators discuss qualitative and quantitative data collection processes, referring to methodologies employed. Processes in which the data are collected using rather rigorous instrumentation might be referred to as quantitative. The use of tests, especially standardized or norm-referenced tests, would yield quantitative data. The use of observation, interview, or survey in which there is the possibility of much interpretation on the part of either the data collector or the subject would yield qualitative data.

Existing Data

As you decide what kinds of data you need, you will first want to check for existing sources of the data, such as public records. Then you can collect other data you need using instruments such as interview schedules, objective tests and scales, projective tests, and observational analysis.

For the purposes of this book, *public records* is defined more broadly than you may have thought. Of course it includes the public statistics collected by many agencies, such as birth, death, address, and social security numbers. For evaluation, you can also use data in records collected by a variety of agencies, corporations, institutions, community organizations, and the media. For example, an evaluation conducted in a corporation might use payroll records, training records, quality control data, incidence reports, as well as others. An evaluation of a public school adult education program might use government census data to identify whether the correct target population is being served by the program.

The foregoing are examples of antecedent data, or data that have already been collected and stored. As an evaluator, you need to search out such existing data, decide on their usefulness to the evaluation, and figure out how to record them. Specifically, it is these recording devices that become your data source. For example, you may decide it is important to use the training records of all employees over the past five years to examine the effectiveness of the human resources unit in helping to promote the company's five-year strategic plan. Particularly, you are interested in the topics of training activities, which employees completed the activities, and how employees were selected to participate. As the evaluator, you would design a data collection form that would facilitate your recording information as you analyze these training records. Importantly, you need to have a means to record the following for each employee: In what department were they employed (connection to the five-year plan)? What training did they receive (connection to the plan)? When (timeliness)? Was the training completed (effectiveness)? Were employees required to attend or were they given the choice (selection or recruitment)? Was there any pattern to the training completion (connection to the plan)?

Often organizations, both in the public and private sectors, are sensitive to the privacy and confidentiality issues surrounding public records. Because of this, you may either be denied access to such data or be required to collect the data without recording the individual's name. Composite data (totals, averages, and so forth) are usually all that you require, so such restrictions will not be a problem. However, if there needs to be some connection between the individual and the data, as in the example just given, you have your negotiating work ahead of you.

This difficulty is evident in two of the questions based on the evaluation in the Chapter Four scenario of the pharmacist training program:

1. Did those who participated in the program perform significantly better than those who did not?

2. Did supervisors evaluate students' drug audits as being satisfactory?

For the first question, the evaluator might go to the Department of Health records for the scores that people received on state-administered pharmacy licensing tests. The scores of students in this program could then be compared with those of others who were tested but not in the program. For the second question, the evaluator might collect and review the grades that supervisors submitted for students over the previous five years. These scores could be analyzed to see whether any patterns emerged over the time span, and if so, whether the patterns correlate with specific changes in curriculum or faculty.

Questions about using what already exists will always emerge in the evaluation. The evaluator will have to help the staff decide whether existing data will suffice or whether new data need to be collected. An evaluator who is part of the organization will probably know about existing information. An external evaluator needs to ask staff about such information; ideally an atmosphere of participation has been nurtured among staff and they are working partners in the endeavor.

Newly Collected Data

When your evaluation requires data that are not provided by existing sources, you will have to devise or identify ways to collect new evaluation data. You can use a number of methods to collect data, usually defined directly by the nature of the evaluation question, by your access to the data (that is, information provided by staff, students, and others), or by the resources available for the evaluation (time, money, staff). As mentioned earlier, these data sources can be qualitative in nature, such as interviews, surveys, or observational techniques, or quantitative, such as objective tests and scales. See the References at the end of the book for resources with more in-depth discussions of interview techniques, scales, standardized measures, personality measures, and observational analysis.

Interview

You may also gather data from interviews in which questions are asked orally and answers are recorded carefully. Interview schedules or protocols, which are constructed for particular purposes, are what data sources used in interviewing are called. These consist of questions that can take different forms. The structured interview, for example, asks the questions in a particular order, and also provides the answers from which the interviewee chooses. If you use a standardized interview schedule (*standardized* meaning that the way you administer and score it never varies from one time to another, or one interviewer to another), questions are not only ordered in a certain way, but they must also be answered in a specified amount of time. The advantage of such a highly structured interview is its consistency. Presumably, you are seeking certain information from all interviewees and the structured or standardized interview provides the opportunity to get the data you want from all interviewees.

A semistructured interview still provides the questions, but it offers no preexisting answers. The interview, however, is not allowed to wander or become too chatty because you are still constrained by the specific questions that all interviewees must answer. This type of interview sometimes uses a branching process where the interviewer allows the interviewee to respond in a number of directions. However, each direction has a prescribed set of questions that must be followed. This branching may have several levels in which subsequent directions would also have a prescribed set of questions. Obviously, this requires a great deal of preparation and training on the part of the interviewer.

Finally, there is the unstructured interview, in which you have complete freedom to ask any questions. Answers are open-ended. Of course, the interviewer must have a goal for the interview and the questions will necessarily reflect that goal. This interview format is difficult to conduct objectively and therefore requires special training. Because the interviewer can essentially ask any question he or she wants to, the questions' logic and applicability are sometimes in doubt. It is easy to see the extraneous factors that could affect such an interview: the interviewer's excessive talking, unrelated questions, unfocused responses, and answers that are difficult to compare from one interview to another (Gatewood and Feild, 1994).

What kinds of questions are found in the various interview schedules? You will encounter many types among them, including the following:

- Fixed alternative questions whose responses are specific, for example: "Do you feel that the training department is meeting your professional growth needs?" Response: yes/no, or agree/disagree.

- Open-ended questions in which you, the evaluator, ask the question and then allow the interviewee to fill in and elaborate on any answers. A minimum of restraint is imposed and the interviewee may or may not see this lack of restraint as a threat. For example: "Other than computer literacy, supervision, and team building, what are some professional growth needs that the training department might address?"

- Funnel questions start with a broad view of a topic and keep narrowing to a finer point. The technique is also called "branching," as described previously. For example: "Have you participated in a training department–sponsored activity in the past month? Was the training helpful in your immediate job responsibilities? How did you incorporate this new knowledge into your job? What were the results?"

- Scale items in which the interviewer sets the degree or scale. Answers are ranked 1 to 10, from strongly agree to strongly disagree. For example, the items might be set up in this way:

How would you say the training helped you?

Definitely helped and will use

Definitely helped, but can't use at this time

Not very helpful to what I do, but interesting

Totally useless and a waste of my time

Whatever the type of interview questions, there are definite criteria by which you can judge the quality of the questions. Questions must, first of all, be relevant and important. The decision regarding relevance is the evaluator's. The type of question should be suitable to your need: Will open-ended questions be more appropriate than closed ones? Should you use the scaled variety? Second, questions should be unambiguous, not open to other interpretations or double meanings. If you are looking for data on specific areas, then be specific in your questioning. Third, you should include only one idea per item. The use of complex or compound questions will only confuse interviewees and probably cause them to answer in a confusing manner.

Fourth, questions should be devoid of value-laden words, such as "educated people believe" or "as a professional." Fifth, to avoid bias, do not ask any leading questions, such as "Don't you think . . . ?" or "Shouldn't you . . . ?"

Sixth, consider whether the person being interviewed needs special knowledge to answer any of the items. Branch away from the unknown. For example, in an open-ended interview, if you ask, "Do you know what ISO 9000 is?" and the answer is "No," then you need to branch away. Seventh, are you asking for personal information, such as personal family information or private habits? Do so only if it is absolutely necessary and after rapport has been established. Finally, is your question loaded with peer opinions that may influence the answer, such as "According to your fellow employees . . ."? If so, replace them with funneling to get to the point. For example, "Have you talked to your fellow employees about this?" "Do you agree with them?" "If not, why not?"

There are positive and negative aspects to using the interview schedule as a data source. The interview is adaptable to any data collection and useful with all kinds of clients, including those who are physically challenged, do not speak English (use an interpreter), or read poorly or not at all. Furthermore, the interview can take place on the telephone and yet is suited to in-depth information gathering. Interviews can even be performed over the Internet using standard "chat" software. This computer technique can also work well with people who cannot write well or legibly.

As useful as interviews are, one needs to look at the possible problems and at some precautions. Obviously, the interview is as good as the quality of the questions. In addition, interviews are an expensive data source for several reasons: they are time consuming; they require training to do; and the number of people (the sample) that you can interview at any one time is necessarily small. Finally, the unstructured interview may come under scrutiny as its results are sometimes open to interpretation.

As a precaution, you may want to consider an already constructed interview schedule that has a proven record of reliability and validity. You can often find these in other evaluation or research reports that have been published.

Another precaution is to be sure all interviewers are trained and their process of interviewing is standardized. If you are working with a team of interviewers, all should be trained at the same time in order to ensure consistency. In that way, everyone will ask questions in the same way and will learn to record answers objectively. Also, you need to account for inter-rater reliability, that is, the extent to which different raters agree on what they hear. This process can be a very difficult one both to train and to monitor once in process. Sometimes, when you use several interviewers, the strategy is to have only one person go over the notes or transcripts of the interviews. That one person then becomes the rater.

One final precaution: if you are doing telephone interviews, be sure to give the interviewee an opportunity to call back immediately to identify the interviewer. Interviewees need to feel confident that they are giving information to a legitimate interviewer or organization.

Scales

If you need a data source that can measure attitudes, interests, or values, you may choose one of several different types of scales. Scales are a series of gradations that describe and measure something in a ranking way, using symbols, words, or numbers. Three kinds of continuums (scales) that you can use in constructing such instruments are described here.

The *Likert scale* is the one most often used to measure attitudes, interests, and values. It usually starts with a question or a statement, followed by a scaled response. For example:

It is important to be a lifelong learner.

Strongly Agree   Agree   Neither Agree nor Disagree
Disagree   Strongly Disagree

Scales can also be set up with numbers, for example, using 5 for strong agreement down to 1 for strong disagreement. You may also see a Likert scale that gives only four choices or that provides no middle-ground statement, for example, "neither agree or disagree," in order to force the test taker to make a choice. The possible responses might be these: very concerned, concerned, moderately concerned, unconcerned. What is left out? You see no answer that says, "neither concerned nor unconcerned." These are called "forced choice" scales.

In another type of scale called *equal appearing intervals* (Gay, 1995), the respondent chooses one statement out of three or four. Example:

1. I believe that JTPA is the greatest institution for job training in America today.

2. I believe in job training but don't need any.

3. I think JTPA is a hindrance to societal change because it still relies on minimal job skills, minimum wages, and blue-collar jobs.

Although used consistently in social science contexts, the scale presents a problem in that it takes a long time to prepare. In addition, different people may not agree that the intervals are equal. Without agreement on the equality of the intervals, people may suspect the ability of the instrument to accurately measure the construct in question. For example, a five-point scale for grading an instructor associates the number 1 with the least effective performance and the number 5 with the most effective performance. Once the scores are tallied and averaged, the participants may have rated the instructor a 4.6. The argument is this: Although a 4.6 definitely indicates more effectiveness than a 4, what is the specific difference between the rating of 4 as opposed to 5? Some training organizations identify the difference by saying that 4 is effective and 5 is very effective. In this situation, two more questions emerge: How will the participant know what type of instructor performance is truly rated as effective or very effective, and does a score of 3.6 mean that the instructor is one full "effectiveness" rating below someone rated at 4.6?

A *cumulative scale* gathers more detail about what the respondent means by using branching: it asks a question, then stretches the rating as it branches to the next question. Example:

1. Should an indicted politician be allowed to speak at a company's awards night?

2. Would you support his or her campaign?

3. Should donations be collected at the dinner?

The test uses branching to reveal layers of attitude as it moves from the first to the last question.

A value scale called a *semantic differential* places a set of adjective pairs opposite each other, such as

Good /___/___/___/___/___/ Bad

and the test taker indicates a point between the two that shows his or her attitude toward an idea, person, or concept. The pairs represent three categories of adjectives: evaluation (good/bad, clean/dirty), potency (large/small, heavy/light), and activity (active/passive, sharp/dull). A group of these adjective pairs (probably nine to fifteen) would appear under a word or concept, such as "total quality." The responses to the adjective pairs give a measure of the respondent's attitude toward total quality.

Sentence Completion

Sentence completion is an important tool used to measure communication. In this technique, respondents are asked to complete a sentence, a thought, or a problem. They are usually asked to put the answer in their own words. However, you can also provide respondents with some choices, as you will see. There are several formats for sentence completion. One is the *sentence* or *construct construction* in which you pose a situation to the respondents and ask them to come up with a solution. An example might be: "If you were the new personnel director and were asked to settle a dispute between a supervisor who will not release a person for training and that employee, who needs training, what would you do?"

Respondents are asked to answer the question using their own words. You may simply look for the "right" answer. Or you may predesign certain acceptable answers into a rubric with which you can then score the response.

Another format is *completion*, in which the respondent is provided with a partial (incomplete) thought and asked to complete it. An example might be the following: "If I were a personnel director and a supervisor said I could not take an employee for training, I would say to him. . . ." The respondents are asked to complete the sentence with an idea stated in their own words. Scoring might be similar to the previous example.

A third format is *choice*, or *ordering*, in which a scenario is presented and the respondent is asked to select from or rank a list of possible responses. An example would be:

> Of the following responses, which would you use to respond to a supervisor who will not release an employee for needed training?
>
> Do it or die.
>
> It would benefit your operation in the long run.
>
> I have the authority over you.
>
> Why don't you want to release him?
>
> This might lead to an employee grievance filing.

The responses could be analyzed similarly to the other completion formats.

Tests

Another data source consists of objective tests that are standardized measures yielding numerical values. By "standardized," we mean that these tests are administered and scored the same way every time. Evaluators need to know about tests because they are associated with a number of programs and projects. They are important to evaluations of hiring practices as well as to measurements of skills before and after training programs. The scoring of these tests is objective in that specific scoring instructions and test answers are provided by the test maker. In other words, testers do not inject their personal opinions or judgments into the scoring.

Among the standardized tests most frequently administered are mental ability tests and aptitude tests. Some of these tests have been used for many years in schools at all levels and in human resource selection in civilian as well as military environments. The tests give results for cognitive abilities including verbal skills, math skills, and psychomotor abilities.

Another type of objective test is the achievement test. Achievement tests give you a way of measuring current proficiency in a certain area. In other words, what has an employee learned as a result of a course in computer programming, or math, or English, or what does a prospective trainee already know that can be measured? Additionally, you need to know that achievement tests are either norm- or criterion-referenced.

The norm-referenced test is standardized or "normed" on many scores. The results or score of an individual would be compared to the scores of others (like him or her) who have already completed the test. That individual's score is then measured against a percentile range of functioning of the norm group to determine relative levels of functioning. Sponsors like a discussion of norm-referenced tests in evaluations because they compare the scores of individuals in one program to those in other programs.

The criterion-referenced achievement test indicates how a program compares to some standard of performance established by those who developed the program. For example, a staff first decides on standards applicable to blueprint reading and then prepares a test based on the standard. The problem is that whoever prepares the test needs proficiency in creating such an instrument.

Personality measures compose another group of standardized tests. Some of the tests need to be administered and scored by trained counselors, and the objective is to identify behaviors that are not "normal." Such tests measure an individual's enduring traits, traits such as self-concept, or traits that paint a picture of a person. Similar to the procedure for norm-referenced achievement tests, norms are generated from large populations of test takers to establish certain parameters for the traits being tested. For instance, the Minnesota Multiphasic Personality Inventory (MMPI) may be administered to prospective employees to determine whether they possess certain traits that are either beneficial or detrimental to the job.

Projective tests, mentioned earlier, are also a type of personality measure. They evaluate the structure of personality by looking at a person's response to a stimulus, such as the Rorschach test's use of a picture. In an evaluation, such data sources may be useful in determining whether the program of recruitment of individuals was effective. However, administering this type of instrument requires special skills, abilities, and practice, and may be beyond what you need to accomplish. Still, you need to know about these instruments if they have been used in a program or project you are evaluating.

Easier-to-use personality assessments do not give as much information, but they do give insight into a part of the personality, for example, learning style, ability to motivate oneself, self-concept, and so forth. Evaluators can easily learn to use and evaluate the results.

Observational Analysis

In observational analysis, you record objectively by using open-ended (narrative) response formats or predetermined response formats such as scales or categories of behavior. This technique can be time-intensive and either obtrusive or unobtrusive. "Obtrusive" means that individuals being measured know that you are collecting data about or from them. "Unobtrusive" means that the individuals have no idea that you are measuring them.

Obtrusive observational analysis is used by an evaluator to assess program delivery (Wholey, Hatrey, and Newcomer, 1994). It may involve an observer watching and recording what he or she sees, either using a form or narratively, using pen and paper. Or the person being observed may be filmed or taped while answering questions or performing some task. The key is that the person knows that he or she is being observed, even if that person doesn't know the reason.

Unobtrusive observational analysis is simply the opposite. The individual has no idea that he or she is the focus of data collection, or that data are even being collected. The most popular example of this format is the hidden camera or audio recorder.

Analysis of these data would be similar to the methods described for interviews, scales, and sentence completion.

Putting It All Together

In this chapter we discussed the "means" by which evaluators collect and record the information necessary to address their evaluation questions. Often these means, usually referred to as data sources, are already in place as part of the program being evaluated. Program planners frequently design data collection processes and instruments into their activities. Often data collection design is performed more to collect monitoring data than as part of an evaluation design. A good evaluator can uncover these existing data sources and figure out how they might be used or "tweaked" to yield data needed in the evaluation. Where that is not the case, the evaluator needs to know how to design, adopt, or adapt other data sources.

Questions and Exercise

Now that you have read Chapter Six, return to the questions that you were asked to keep in mind at the beginning of the chapter.

1. What are the differences between qualitative and quantitative?
2. What are the levels of data that you might encounter?
3. What are some instruments that you might use or develop?

Answer those questions in two ways:

- Write a general answer that applies to the chapter material.
- Use your new understanding to write a specific answer that applies to the scenario. Be sure to address these issues:

What data sources will support the evaluation of the proposed gardening program?

Can you predict how data will be collected in the gardening program quantitatively? How about qualitatively?

Exercise

Return to your own project, detailed in Chapter One. What data sources will you use in your evaluation? Enter them on a chart of the evaluation design format like the one in Exhibit 6.1.

Further Reading

Zemke, R., and Kramlinger, T. *Figuring Things Out: A Trainer's Guide to Needs and Task Analysis*. Reading, Mass.: Addison-Wesley, 1982.

EXHIBIT 6.1 Evaluation Design Format.

Evaluation Question	Activities to Observe	Data Source	Population Sample	Data Collection Design	Responsibility	Data Analysis	Audience

7

Data Analysis

SCENARIO 7   Mike Ramirez called the program committee meeting to order—this time with a certain dread. He knew what Judy's topic was for this meeting, and although he was fairly comfortable with it, he could predict the screams of agony when the staff heard these words: "number crunching." Judy smiled, but sympathetically, when she saw Mike's discomfort. She was familiar with this reaction, had seen and dealt with it many, many times. For now, Judy could only reassure him that "number crunching" was, in fact, understandable to all those present *and did not necessarily mean that they would be dealing with "real numbers."* She explained that she would begin with a few definitions of essential terms—what is a statistic?—and then move on to simple examples of working with data. They would revisit a topic introduced at the last meeting about data sources, that is, nominal, ordinal, interval, and ratio levels. Judy predicted that the group would be surprised that, unknowingly, they had been engaged in the first steps that prepared them for simple "number crunching." Now the committee needed to know exactly what to do with the data they were about to gather.

Judy reminded Mike of other important reasons for learning to handle the data. Importantly, their grant application had a much better chance of being accepted for funding if they made the commitment to "crunching the numbers." Indeed, the Cox Foundation would be looking for the interpretation that the data would yield: the efficiency, effectiveness, and impact of the gardening program.

Think about the following questions as you read Chapter Seven:

1. What are data?
2. What are the main terms evaluators need to know in order to analyze data?
3. How do mean, median, and mode (measures of central tendency) offer different perspectives on data sets?

When you finish reading, you should be able to answer the questions as they relate to the preceding scenario as well as to the chapter material.

Key Words and Concepts

Statistic: A number or characteristic; also, a tool or technique

Measure of central tendency: A single score that characterizes a set of scores, that is, the mode, median, or mean

Measures of variability (range and standard deviation): Statistical tests used to determine how much scores in a set differ from or are similar to one another

Data

The term *data* usually conjures the image of numerical figures that are presented in a table or graph, after having been manipulated using some complex formula. Although that image in fact is true, data can also take on other forms. Responses to interview questions (narrative), survey items (scales), and observations (narrative or counts) are all considered data. Like numbers, once these data are collected they need to be analyzed systematically and objectively in order to yield meaningful information for the program evaluation. The data can be analyzed using a variety of different data analysis (statistical) procedures.

In a face-to-face interview, for example, the evaluator is the data collector, using an interview schedule (instrument). The evaluator asks a question, immediately analyzes the response, and if necessary redirects the interviewee to another topic or asks for a fuller explanation. Careful notes are kept from which information is culled that is pertinent to the evaluation questions. This is a process called "coding" (Babbie, 1989). There are now computer programs that do the coding for qualitative evaluation.

Observations can take place unobtrusively, as the evaluator gathers information, for example, about the setting of a program or about the interactions among people (Wholey, Hatry, and Newcomer, 1994). Information can be recorded in two ways: The evaluator can record careful, detailed notes on the observations, which will later be coded. Or, if there are specific items or attributes that the evaluator needs to track in order to answer the evaluation question, then a list or guide might be developed beforehand to be checked off during the observations. This becomes, in effect, a rating scale.

In other programs observations may be conducted obtrusively, as described in Chapter Six; the evaluator may even become one of the participants.

The prospect of having to do statistical work can produce sweaty palms for many of us. But here is the good news: you no longer need to know how to crunch numbers to produce valuable statistics. There are simple computer programs that can perform that task, easily and affordably. (See the Software and Further Reading lists at the end of the chapter.) One need only be aware of a few basic concepts about the analyzed data.

Terms

What do you do with the data you have collected? How do you get the numbers crunched? In order to answer those questions, you need some information and definitions. Newcomers to evaluation find the task of data analysis the most intimidating part of the evaluation process. In this chapter we will try to demystify this process and give you some basic skills to use in your role as an evaluator. A better understanding of this chapter's key words will be the first step.

Statistics

The term *statistic* can refer to two types of things: a number or characteristic, or a tool or technique. Numbers that describe certain attributes of Mr. Smith, such as weight, height, performance on a test, or five-year baseball batting average are statistics that can be applied to individuals or groups.

As a tool, a statistic can also represent a mathematical formula applied to a group of numbers to obtain an attribute of individuals or groups that are meaningful to the evaluation. The formula may also be applied over a period of time, and to the group that Mr. Smith belongs to, as well as across all members, and to compare Mr. Smith's group with another group. Thus this second definition refers to the statistical analysis of a set of data.

Measures of Central Tendency

Whenever a set of data presents itself in an evaluation, a first impulse is to simplify the data set into an easily understandable number that is relatively descriptive of the numbers in the set. This number becomes useful and meaningful regardless of whether you are dealing with a small or large sample. Such a number is one of the *measures of central tendency*, or a point at which a sample (data) is split in half. Measures of central tendency give you different ways of summarizing numbers. This chapter covers three measures of central tendency, all of which you have used in simple contexts.

Look at the following data on the patients of a health maintenance organization (HMO) and the number of dental hygiene visits made by each in the past twenty-four months. We will use these data to illustrate the three measures.

Patient Name	A	B	C	D	E	F	G	H	I
Number of Cleanings	0	2	2	1	3	1	4	3	3

This list presents a statistic for each participant in the group. But if you wish to discuss the group as a whole, there are several ways to do so: using an average (or mean), a median, or a mode. Each method of analysis offers a different perspective on the whole group.

Mode. Assume that the HMO has a program whose goal is to see every patient twice a year for teeth cleaning. Is there a way to summarize this information, using one number, in order to determine whether the goal has been reached? One way would be to ask what number of cleanings occurs most frequently. But to answer the question, you would probably want to set up the information in a different way, that is, show the cleanings in increasing numbers from 0 to 4.

Patient Name	A	D	F	B	C	E	H	I	G
Number of Cleanings	0	1	1	2	2	3	3	3	4

Setting up the list in this way shows frequency more readily. As you can see, the number that occurs most often is 3. Thus 3 is the *mode* for this data set, or one measure of central tendency.

The mode is the appropriate measure when you are working with the nominal data in the chart. What would happen if you calculated an average for this data set? As you will see later, the average is 2.1. Now consider the nature of the data set, which is the number of times individuals had their teeth cleaned. Is it appropriate to think about 2.1 cleanings? No. If the HMO wanted to use the analysis to determine how often its patients were using the HMO's resources, then an exact number of the most frequently occurring number of visits would be more meaningful.

Another example of the mode, or most frequently occurring number, appears in a list of scores. Perhaps you administered a scale of attitudes toward teamwork and organized the scores in ascending order. The ten scores were 14, 16, 17, 17, 17, 18, 21, 19, 20, 21. What score occurred most often? Yes, 17 is the mode, and it gives the evaluator a fast accounting of the team's attitudes. But the mode does not necessarily have to be a number. If you had a set of data on religious affiliation and the responses were 4 identified as Protestant, 3 as Catholic, 8 as Jewish, and 2 as Hindu, the mode of this data set would be Jewish.

Mean. Another measure is the *mean*, the mathematical average of a group of numbers, or of a set of data, calculated (in the earlier example) by summing up all the teeth cleanings and dividing by the number of subjects. All of the cleanings add up to 19. Divide by 9 patients and the answer is a mean of 2.1. Another very simple example is one in which scores on a test given after training are 80, 90, 75, 85, and 95. To calculate the mean, you sum up the scores (425) and divide by the number of scores (425 divided by 5 equals 85). The mean score is 85. Obviously, you can't have a mean for the religion data set in the previous example.

Median. Our last measure of central tendency is the *median*. It is, simply, the middle point in a data set. Look once again at the group of patient numbers in ascending order:

0 1 1 2 2 3 3 3 4

In this group of numbers, the middle one is the fifth one (2), leaving four numbers on each side of it.

What happens if there is an even number of values? If the visits of patient D are removed from the chart, the list becomes

0 1 1 2 3 3 3 4

Now two numbers share the physical middle, that is, 2 and 3. The median becomes the midpoint between those two numbers, or 2.5. If we had removed the score of patient E instead, the data set would have been

0 1 1 2 2 3 3 4

The midpoint would now fall between the two scores of 2. Thus, the median would be 2.

The interesting point to observe here is that given the same data set on patient teeth cleanings, you have a different number for the central tendency depending on which measure you use: the mode (3), the mean (2.1), or the median (2). The median is the most appropriate to use with ordinal data. Because ordinal data are basically scale data (1 through 5, or Strongly Agree to Strongly Disagree), you would want to know the midpoint in the data set to scale responses. If the same data were responses to the question "How satisfied are you with the teeth cleaning services of this HMO?" the results might look like Table 7.1. If you rank-ordered these responses, the fifth score (midpoint in a set of nine patient responses) would be 2, or a median of 2. This means that the respondents tended to be satisfied with the services.

Measures of Variability

Measures of variability refers to the different statistical tests that you might employ to discover how much the scores in a data set differ or

TABLE 7.1 Patient Friendly Program.

Patient	Very Satisfied	◄———————————►			Very Dissatisfied
	1	2	3	4	5
A		X			
B	X				
C		X			
D			X		
E		X			
F		X			
G			X		
H	X				
I					X

are similar to one another. Common measures are the interquartile range and the standard deviation.

Ranges, Quartiles, and Percentiles. *Range* is probably the simplest measure of variability to understand. It is just the difference between the lowest score and the highest score in a response set. For example, suppose you have a set of scores, 25, 26, 37, 60, 71, 79, 88, 90, and 95. The range is 95 – 25 = 70. The range for this set is 70. In the set 5, 5, 7, 7, 7, 8, 9, 9, the range is 4. The way you read the range is this: If the range is small, the scores are close together. If the range is large, the scores are more spread out. Obviously, the range is not a very rigorous measure of variability and you should probably use it only to get a "quick and dirty" estimate of variability.

A helpful method of describing individual scores on a test or survey is to employ percentiles, sometimes referred to as centiles. A percentile shows a particular measurement's position in a group in terms of the percentage of measurements falling below it.

A range of measurements may be divided into the 25th, 50th, 75th, and 100th percentiles. These four quartiles represent the *inter-*

quartile range. An instrument (standardized test) developer collects scores from a wide variety of individuals on a particular instrument and divides the scores into the four quartiles. Depending on the instrument and the population it is administered to, different scores will fall into the different quartiles. Thus a score of 75 out of a possible 100 does not necessarily fall into the 75th percentile. Depending on how well or poorly the group performed, that score of 75 might be in the 50th or 100th percentile.

For example, a person completing a standardized writing skills test given to all candidates for employment at XYZ Corporation may receive a score of 65 out of 100. At first glance a score of 65 seems abysmal, but when compared to the scores received by others on the same test, it might not be bad at all. If, for example, the score of 65 falls into the 75th percentile, that means the test taker exceeded the scores of 75 percent of the standardization group.

Sometimes the quartiles are expanded into percentiles so that the scale now includes 95th, 90th, and so forth, with smaller ranges of score values attributed to each one.

Standard Deviation and Variance. Our other measure of variability, the *standard deviation*, is the point at which 34 percent of the sample (data set) falls on either side of the mean. If you have a set of ten scores on a training exam (4 5 3 2 8 3 3 5 3 4) and you are interested in knowing not only the mean (4) but also the range of scores where 34 percent of your group fell below the mean and 34 percent above, you would calculate the standard deviation. You might ask why an evaluator would need to know such a thing, and this is the answer: if an evaluator is interested in determining the spread of scores on an activity by looking at just one number, he or she could use the standard deviation.

Suppose a test has been administered that had a possible score range of 0 to 10. Looking at the mean, you would assume that your group tended to get half of the test items correct. However, looking at the standard deviation of the data set (1.6) you would now know that 34 percent of the group scored between 2.4 and 4.0, and that 34 percent of the group scored between 4.0 and 5.6. Also, you would see that the majority (68 percent) scored between 2.4 and 5.6 on the test. This may imply that the trainees need much more work on this material before they will understand it.

You can get the formula to calculate the standard deviation in any good research or statistics book. (See the Further Reading list at the end of this chapter.) However, we recommend getting a good statistical analysis computer program and letting the machine do the calculating for you.

The *variance* is the square of the standard deviation and represents a kind of average of the distance of the individual scores from the mean of the set of scores. The larger the variance, the greater the variability, or distance, from the mean.

Levels of Data

Now we can return to a topic you learned about in Chapter Six: levels of data. Do you recall these terms: nominal, ordinal, interval, and ratio? Data exist in a number of forms and depending on how you, the evaluator, decide to measure these data, you will use one or more of these levels.

For example, if the HMO wanted to know the numbers of men and of women in the list of dental cleaning visits, then nominal data would be sufficient for the purpose. The data collector would add another column of data in which each person is identified by gender, as done in Table 7.2. As you can see, in this nominal format the patients can belong to only one of two categories: male or female. The data reveal that there are four males and five females. Other nominal data may involve many categories, for example, age ranges (such as sixteen to thirty, thirty-one to fifty, fifty-one to sixty-five), ethnic background, country of origin, and so forth.

An additional round of data gathering might ask, "In which New England states do our clients reside?" Table 7.3 shows the results. How can you summarize the data? One way is to say that more than double the number of clients are residents of Massachusetts—

TABLE 7.2 Patient Information.

Patient	Number of Cleanings	Gender
A	0	Male
B	2	Female
C	2	Female
D	1	Female
E	3	Male
F	1	Female
G	4	Male
H	3	Male
I	3	Female

five of the nine—in comparison to each of the other states. You can also report that the mode for patients is Massachusetts. This and other demographics may be important information in the monitoring of your program or project.

The next level of measurement, ordinal, ranks objects or individuals on a variable. Categories are compared to each other and results are expressed in "more than" or "less than" terms. Importantly, however, this kind of scale does not assume equal distance between the categories. For example, suppose ten people are asked on a posttest how they would rank their overall satisfaction with their dentist. The following results show that 30 percent of the population answered "Satisfied," but we do not know the degree of separation between, for example, Satisfied and Strongly Satisfied.

Response	Number	Percent
5: Highly satisfied	1	10
4: Satisfied	3	30
3: Neutral	0	0
2: Dissatisfied	4	40
1: Highly dissatisfied	2	20

TABLE 7.3 Patient Information.

Patient	Number of Cleanings	Gender	Residence
A	0	Male	Connecticut
B	2	Female	Massachusetts
C	2	Female	Rhode Island
D	1	Female	Massachusetts
E	3	Male	Massachusetts
F	1	Female	Rhode Island
G	4	Male	Massachusetts
H	3	Male	Connecticut
I	3	Female	Massachusetts

In the data set, what percentage of the population (10 people) surveyed were satisfied with the dentist? The answer is 40 percent (10 percent highly satisfied plus 30 percent satisfied). However, 20 percent were highly dissatisfied, 0 percent neutral, and 40 percent dissatisfied. Because of the nature of ordinal data (no assumption of equal intervals between the categories), to examine the data in any way other than the percentage of responses in each category is inappropriate.

For example, if you were to calculate the mean of the responses, it would be 2.7 ($1 \times 5 + 3 \times 4 + 0 \times 3 + 4 \times 2 + 2 \times 1 = 27/10 = 2.7$). What does 2.7 indicate when you are looking at an ordinal scale ranging from Highly Satisfied to Highly Dissatisfied? Does it mean that the respondents tended to be almost neutral? In truth, it is difficult to make any sense of it at all. However, if you want to see if these satisfaction ratings changed after implementing the new Patient Friendly Program, you could compare the patient group's pretest and posttest numbers in Table 7.4.

TABLE 7.4 Patient Satisfaction Before and After
Patient Friendly Program.

Response	Pretest Number	Pretest Percent	Posttest Number	Posttest Percent
5: Highly satisfied	2	20	4	40
4: Satisfied	4	40	4	40
3: Neutral	1	10	0	0
2: Dissatisfied	2	20	1	10
1: Highly dissatisfied	1	10	1	10

You can see that there has been some change in patient satisfaction with the dentist. Was this change attributable to the new Patient Friendly Program? You would like to think so.

The next level of measurement is interval. Interval scales are like the ordinal in that they rank-order information, but they add an important characteristic: the assumption of equal intervals between numbers. Still, there is no absolute zero. For example, on a 100-item test on business process quality, Sean answered 40 questions correctly, Joanna 60, David 80, and Maria 100. Looking at these numbers, we can say that there is a 20-point spread between any two nearest individual test scores. We can also say that David doubled Sean's score and that Maria answered every question correctly. Why can we say that? In this case, the intervals between the numbers are equal. However, if Matthew took the test and scored a zero, we could not say that he knew nothing at all about business process quality because there is no absolute zero at this level of measurement. Matthew knows a number of things about flow charting, cycle time, inputs, outputs, and so forth. He just failed to correctly answer any of the questions on this particular test (Gatewood and Feild, 1990).

You can also report on the group performance of Sean, Joanna, David, and Maria as having a mean score of 70 because of the assumption about equal intervals. That is, you can analyze the data arithmetically.

Sometimes people create ordinal scales and mistakenly treat them as interval data. For instance, look at the following scale wherein quality of work is compared in "more than" and "less than" terms.

Quality of Work: The Extent to Which the Employee Actually Completes Job Assignment Correctly

1: Almost always makes errors; has very low accuracy

2: Quite often makes errors

3: Makes errors but equals job standards

4: Makes a few errors; has high accuracy

5: Almost never makes errors; has very high accuracy

In order to consider these as interval data, the evaluator would need to build a rationale that justifies considering the interval between the 1 and the 2 equal to the interval between the 4 and the 5. Now look at the following version of the scale to see how this can be done.

1: Almost always makes errors; has very low accuracy. Commits 25 or more errors in a month.

2: Quite often makes errors. Commits 18–24 errors in a month.

3: Makes errors but equals job standards. Commits 11–17 errors in a month.

4: Makes a few errors; has high accuracy. Commits 5–10 errors in a month.

5: Almost never makes errors; has very high accuracy. Commits 0–4 errors in a month.

As you see, the evaluator has identified what number of errors would coincide with the five categories. If a person commits 25 errors or more in a month, the quality of work is a category 1; if 18–24, a category 2, and so forth. Then you have created a scale that is in fact based on interval data.

If the assumption of equal intervals between scale items is not established, then one would be misled to believe that a calculated mean of 2.2 means that it is 10 segments in the scale less than a mean of 3.2.

Finally, we have the ratio level of measurement. Ratio data sets are distinguished by equal intervals between the values and an absolute zero value. A list of heights or weights, for example, can start with zero—no weight or height at all—and progress from there. Likewise, there are equal intervals between temperatures, which allows you to say that the temperature in freezer A (20 degrees Fahrenheit) is twice as cold as the temperature in freezer B (40 degrees Fahrenheit). Other ratio scales would be time, distance, and speed. You can consider, for example, the concept of no time between two events. Yet, with the absolute zero point, you can measure from 0 to 1 and say that this interval is equal to the interval between 8 and 9. Also, with the absolute zero point, you can talk about negative numbers and assume that the interval between two negative numbers is equal to the interval between two positive numbers, or that freezer C at –20 degrees Fahrenheit is three times as cold as freezer B at +40 degrees Fahrenheit.

For the most part, evaluation and behavioral research collect and analyze nominal, ordinal, and interval data. Seldom do we deal with ratio data.

You may have questions that come up as you look closely at your data sources, data collection, and data analysis. For example, which analysis procedures are most appropriate given the level of data? Also, what does it mean if the statistical software indicates that the findings are not significant? For an in-depth explanation, see the Appendix. Also, consult one or more of the books suggested in this chapter's Further Reading list.

Putting It All Together

Many people see data analysis as something mystical and far too complex for them to comprehend. In truth, the secret to effective data analysis is in knowing which statistic is best, given (1) your level of data (nominal, ordinal, interval, or ratio) and (2) which statistical procedure is warranted given the question you are trying to answer. A computer can perform the actual analysis. In fact, a computer should perform it. You just need to be aware of the different tools that you have at your beck and call to apply to the evaluation design.

Finally, you need to understand and interpret the statistic that will emerge from the analysis. Being able to draw inferences and conclusions about the efficiency, effectiveness, and impact of a program from a mere number is a powerful talent.

Questions and Exercise

Now that you have read Chapter Seven, return to the questions that you were asked to keep in mind at the beginning of the chapter.

1. What are data?
2. What are the main terms evaluators need to know in order to analyze data?
3. How do mean, median, and mode (measures of central tendency) offer different perspectives on data sets?

Answer those questions in two ways:

- Write a general answer that applies to the chapter material.
- Use your new understanding to write a specific answer that applies to the scenario. Be sure to address this issue:

  Identify what level(s) of data will apply to the gardening program's evaluation. Defend your answer with examples.

Exercise

Insert your data analysis decisions from the preceding questions into a chart like the one in Exhibit 7.1.

Further Reading

Fitz-Gibbon, C. T., and Morris, L. L. *How to Calculate Statistics*. Newbury Park, Calif.: Sage Publications, 1987.

Freedman, D., Pisani, R., and Purves, R. *Statistics*. (3rd ed.) New York: W. W. Norton & Co., 1998.

Graham, A. *Statistics*. Chicago: NTC/Contemporary, 1994.

Norman, G. R., and Streiner, D. L. *PDQ Statistics*. St. Louis: Mosby, 1997.

Patton, M. Q. *How to Use Qualitative Methods in Evaluation*. Newbury Park, Calif.: Sage, 1987.

Zemke, R., and Kramlinger, T. *Figuring Things Out: A Trainer's Guide to Needs and Task Analysis*. Reading, Mass.: Addison-Wesley, 1982.

Software for Personal Computers

SAS Institute, Inc. "StatView for Mac." Cary, N.C.: SAS Institute, 1999.

SAS Institute, Inc. "StatView for Windows." Cary, N.C.: SAS Institute, 1999.

SPSS, Inc. "SPSS 6.1 for Macintosh." Chicago: SPSS, Inc., 1990.

SPSS, Inc. "SPSS 9.0 for Windows." Chicago: SPSS, Inc., 1995.

SPSS, Inc. "Systat 8.0 Student Version." Chicago: SPSS, Inc., 1999.

EXHIBIT 7.1 Evaluation Design Format.

Evaluation Question	Activities to Observe	Data Source	Population Sample	Data Collection Design	Responsibility	Data Analysis	Audience

8

Is It Evaluation or Is It Research?

SCENARIO 8   During the last conversation between the evaluation consultant, Judy Hallowell, and the Grandview staff, Luis asked, "Well, how do we do this research?" Judy surprised many in the group by asking them if they thought they were going to be involved in research or in evaluation. Especially after their long discussion about "number crunching," a number of staff members said, "Well, of course we are doing research." Others asked, "How do we really know if we're doing research or evaluation?" Actually, these questions gave Judy the perfect opportunity to make some important distinctions between evaluation and research.

Once again, she asked the committee to form small working and discussion groups. In this format, they were more likely to explore the ideas that Judy felt they should delve into. She asked the groups to think about and discuss what they felt was their main intent in doing the evaluation. From a far corner of the room came a voice, "To get the grant money, of course." After the laughter subsided, all agreed that, although obtaining those resources was important, they probably had a more encompassing intent. Just to get the conversations started in the groups, Judy threw out this question: "What is it that you and all your stakeholders want to know the most about—program processes, outcomes of program processes, or ramifications of the program?"

With that intriguing question, the groups began their discussions.

Think about the following questions as you read Chapter Eight:

1. What are the differences between evaluation and research?
2. Why might an evaluator want to use a sample of individuals instead of all individuals?
3. What are the kinds of sampling?

When you finish reading, you should be able to answer the questions as they relate to the preceding scenario as well as to the chapter material.

Key Words and Concepts

Generalizability: Ability to use the results in other settings, with other people

Population: The group—of people or things—from which a sample is taken or about which conclusions are drawn

Sample: The group or people from whom data are gathered

Random sample: The result of choosing from a population in which each member had an equal chance of being chosen

Determining Evaluation or Research from Intent

Are you engaged in research or evaluation? You can answer this question by looking at either your original intent for the evaluation or the evaluation design. The easier of the two to determine is your intent, so we will discuss that first. What is it that you want the results of the evaluation to help the program staff or sponsors to do?

First, you might want to help them examine and better understand the processes that occurred during the program cycle.

Second, you might also, or only, want them to better understand the outcome(s) of those processes.

Third, your intent might be to help them better understand the long-term ramifications of those outcomes and their relationship to what is already known in the professional literature.

If your main intent is the first, then you are probably performing an evaluation and not research, because your focus is on collecting information on the processes while they are in action and providing immediate feedback to the stakeholders. This feedback might be used to compare interim products to a benchmark, identify activities that are or are not working as anticipated, or help the stakeholders assess whether they think the end goals will be met. Your plans are to collect information with the guidance of your evaluation questions, and the questions in turn have been framed so that their answers will help people to better understand the program, its processes, and its intentions. Having been thus enlightened, ideally they will be able to use the evaluation findings to fix or improve the program as needed.

If your main intent is the second, to help staff and sponsors better understand the outcome(s) of the program, then you might be performing evaluation, research, or evaluation-research. You are working to first understand the purposes (expected outcomes) of the program, and then to understand to what extent those purposes have been accomplished. As an evaluator, you can use qualitative or quantitative processes to make these determinations and employ rather rigorous designs to collect data. Your balance point in the evaluation-research continuum depends on your target audience for the results, and their purpose. If the audience is the program staff and sponsor who will use the information to improve the program in the next cycle or continue to fund this program, you are probably performing an evaluation. But if the target audience is the sponsor or members of the professional field who want insight into how they might improve practice across similar programs or promote this process to other programs, you are probably performing research. Or if you are testing or examining processes to be used in the evaluation of other such programs and outcomes, you are probably performing evaluation-research.

If your main intent is the third, to promote understanding of the project's long-term effects and expand what is known in the professional field, then you are probably performing research. Here your focus is to collect data on the existence of a causal link between specific program processes and overall impact on individuals or institutions. You might have as an audience the clients, program staff, sponsors, community, or the profession. However, as a researcher, your intent is to validate the connection of certain actions (the program) to certain observed reactions (your measurements or results) so that the actions might be accepted and possibly adopted by others wishing to experience the same results. Such work often adds more insight into what is already understood in the research literature.

So which is it going to be? You need to look at characteristics of both evaluation and research in order to answer this question. By now, you know that evaluation tries to learn what is going on in a program so the program stakeholders can use the information to improve the program. In research you are trying to expand knowledge for a group well beyond the stakeholders.

Determining Evaluation or Research from Design

Another means to determine whether you are performing evaluation or research is to look at the evaluation design. By looking at how you intend to collect data (data collection design) and the individuals from whom you collect the data (population and sample), you can get a very good idea in which direction you are leaning.

How is the research process different from evaluation? First, in research there is a deliberate attempt to collect data under controlled conditions; true experimental designs are carried out in laboratories. Research leads toward the development of knowledge; you are "stretching the envelope." Using the scientific method, the researcher tries to explain and predict phenomena by controlling variables.

In research, the assumption is that all variables (behaviors) can be controlled and that there are discoverable causes for phenomena found by establishing cause-and-effect relationships. Research is an orderly process. As a researcher, you strive to maintain complete control over all aspects of your design. This, of course, is not easily done in real life. Clients drop in and out of programs and staff changes again and again, to cite only two non-research-friendly occurrences. In addition, under research conditions you try to randomly select participants from the population, and then randomly assign them to either receive or not receive certain treatments (training, education, or service, for example).

Second, in research, unlike evaluation, you can manipulate the variables: change the treatment (for example, a new machine or process in a plant), change the machine or the process in a plant, decide who takes part in the program (for example, all females who are left-handed and blonde), decide where and when it will take place (between May 1 and July 30). Changes to these variables are minimal and controlled. This gives the researcher power and the research design its rigorousness. Without this control, one has diminished power, and thus diminished ability to assess a cause-and-effect relationship. Evaluation, in contrast, provides information so that programs can change. Determining a cause-and-effect relationship is no more of a priority than providing program improvement feedback.

A third condition of research involves establishing the cause-and-effect relationship. As stated earlier, research is an attempt to identify and substantiate causal links between processes and results. The more rigorous the research design, the more sure one can be about inferring causal links from the data. Once such links are made, the researcher can add to the literature so that others may benefit from this new knowledge.

Loss of any of these three conditions means that you no longer have a true experimental design but may have a quasi-experimental design. Although such a design is still experimental, you have lost some of the rigor and consequently some of the ability to infer causal links. For example, say you have three groups that you will be working with, but participants have not been randomly selected or assigned to the groups. Instead, you have what is referred to as a *convenience sample*. You can conduct research that may allow you to establish a cause-and-effect link, but generalizing that link beyond the group of individuals in your study would be inappropriate.

If you have lost two of the conditions required in the research process, you have an *ex post facto design*, which is no longer experimental but rather correlational research. You can still collect new data or you may use existing data such as company records. You will probably have intact groups of subjects, that is, with no random selection or assignment. With a correlational study, you can't infer a cause-and-effect relationship. You can, however, make connections between what you observe (the gender of individuals who enroll in a class) and certain occurrences (those who score in the 90th percentile).

What does all this mean? Simply that if you are conducting an evaluation, you will probably use a correlational, or at best a quasi-experimental, design. And if you are conducting straight research, you can use any of the three forms of design— experimental, quasi-experimental, or correlational—but you will strive for a true experimental design.

Qualitative and Quantitative Characteristics

Another basis for understanding evaluation and research is one that considers whether you are involved with qualitative or quantitative data. As discussed in Chapters One, Six, and Seven, qualitative data concentrate on verbal descriptions, observations, and note taking. *Qualitative* can also describe the manner in which data are gathered (for example, observations, surveys, and interviews).

Qualitative data are primarily at the nominal and ordinal levels. Recall that nominal data are concept specific (categorized as male or female, driving or taking public transport to work, and so forth). Although ordinal data can be ranked, there is no way to measure the magnitude of difference between the rankings. Chapter Seven demonstrated this idea of magnitude of difference with a survey of patients' satisfaction with their dentist. You read that 40 percent were satisfied with the dentist, but you still did not know the magnitude of difference between satisfied and any other category. Therefore, as you learned, it was inappropriate to examine the data in any way other than to look at the percentage of responses in each category.

Quantitative data, on the other hand, are structured, hard data, with certain assumptions about their nature and equivalence. This includes interval data (which possess ranking and equal intervals) and ratio data (which are interval data with the added characteristic of an absolute zero point).

Sampling

We have alluded to samples and populations in earlier sections. What these terms refer to are the individuals in your evaluation on whom or from whom you collect data.

If your company of five thousand employees adopts a training program that everyone takes part in, determining whether the program changed behaviors or imparted knowledge and skills to all would be a daunting, if not impossible, task. Sampling allows you to draw inferences from a smaller number of people within the population. Obviously, the population that we are referring to is not one we normally think about, like the population of the United States or the world population. Instead, we are referring to a group of people, a population, about whom we want to generalize. To do that, you select a smaller number from the population and collect data that apply to the group as a whole. This selection of certain individuals from the larger group (the population) is a sample. You can see that the reason for sampling is mainly to save time and resources.

Three types of questions need to be answered before you sample.

1. What are you questioning? What is the purpose for sampling?

When you have these answers, you can begin to identify your sample. Recall that when we discussed manipulating variables to establish cause-and-effect links, we referred to identifying the characteristics of individuals that you might wish to include in the evaluation. For example, if only half of the five thousand employees in the company are involved in the training, only that half of the population of all employees is eligible for sampling.

2. How are you collecting the data?

The answer to that question affects the sample size. If you are compiling existing data from records, you can readily use many of the records. If you are collecting new data from people, you may have to use a smaller size sample. Also, the nature of data collection will have an impact on the size of the sample. If you are interviewing or using an instrument that is rather costly to purchase and score, then it might be too expensive to think of using a large sample.

3. What are you willing to live with—how rigorous must the sample be?

The more confidence you need in the results, the higher the number that should be sampled. In research designs especially, the size of the sample will directly affect your ability to generalize the results beyond your sample. In an evaluation, you are usually more interested in generalizing to the clients being served. If this client group is small, you can use the entire population and obtain greater generalizability. If it is large, then your generalizability will be governed by your sampling procedure.

Here are some guidelines for sample size that may allow you to avoid using a formula: If the population is less than one hundred, use them all. If the population is one hundred to five hundred, use 50 to 75 percent of the sample. If the population is greater than five hundred, use 10 to 25 percent of the sample. However, when precision is a necessity, there are formulas that can be employed; see for example Williams, 1978.

The criteria that you devise to identify the types (characteristics) of individuals you wish to sample will define your sampling frame. Once you have a sampling frame (for example, women, elderly people, college graduates, those who have had safety training), you need to choose a sampling method. You begin by deciding the following: Will it be a *probability sample*, wherein each and every element in a population has an equal opportunity to be selected? Or will you choose a *nonprobability sample* because the population is so vast or so amorphous that there is no equal opportunity of individuals being in the sample? An example of such a vast population is the population of the United States. You can never actually contact every subject who might be in the sample.

Probability Sampling Methods

Probability sampling methods all use random sampling, but they vary in how complex they are to set up, as the following descriptions demonstrate.

1. An example of *simple random selection* is drawing one hundred names from a hat that contains one thousand names. Taking this method a step further, you might put a number on each of the thousand nameslips and select one hundred of those numbers using a table of random numbers. Today, the common way of selecting random numbers from a large population is with a computer. Random numbers allow you to pick a sample with absolutely no biasing effect.

For example, you want to randomly select 80 teachers to interview from a school system's list of 169 teachers. Bias could occur if you put all the elementary teachers' names into a hat first, followed by the secondary teachers' names, and then fail to shake the hat before drawing. If you just draw from the top, there would be a tendency to have more secondary teachers identified in the sample.

2. A *stratified random sample* takes into account specific groups within a population. For example, in polling, you make calls according to proportions in the population. Suppose you were asking this question: "How does this training affect women?" For a population that is 60 percent women and 40 percent men, your sample should reflect that—60 percent women to 40 percent men. If you employ a simple random sample method, the 60-to-40 proportion might not be reflected in the sample. Because the gender characteristic is important to this evaluation, draw 60 percent of the names out of the women's pile and 40 percent out of the men's pile.

3. A *systematic random sample* requires two things: (a) a population that is well defined, for example one thousand subjects numbered 1 to 1,000, and (b) a clear percentage of the population you wish to have in the sample, such as a 25 percent sample. Using this percentage, you then identify a skip interval. If you are looking for a 25 percent sample out of a population of 1,000, you are looking for 250 individuals. Divide 1,000 by 250 and you get a skip interval of 4. Start anywhere in the list, for example with number 32, and then skip 4 to number 36, 40, 44, and so forth. This is an efficient, effective, and somewhat precise method. One caution is not to alphabetize names before you begin the process, because it might bias your sample.

4. A *cluster random sample* is used for extremely large or even infinite populations. You begin by identifying existing populations, such as voting districts or households or neighborhoods, and then draw samples from the groups that are important to your sampling frame. Some consider this method highly imprecise and arbitrary because it eliminates individuals from being selected because of grouping.

5. A *multistage random sample* is used with very large populations. Your evaluation of a national school-to-work program iden-

tifies a population of 100,000 students. Conventional wisdom says that you need a 10 percent sample, or 10,000. You draw this sample using one of the preceding methods, but your budget can't afford to sample that many. So you draw a 10 percent sample of names from the 10,000 (1,000), but even that number is beyond your budget, so you draw another 10 percent sample from the 1,000 for a new sample of 100. The assumptions of multistage sampling say you can consider this sample of 100 as representative of the population of 100,000. With each reduction in sample size, however, you lose precision and some experts will say that you are pushing the extremes of sampling theory.

Nonprobability Sampling Methods

The results of nonprobability samples are less generalizable, but if that fact doesn't conflict with your purposes, you may find the following sampling methods convenient.

1. A *judgment sample* is one in which you get data from subjects who are selected because of their availability. The subject may be a person on the street or someone on the plant floor, or a group that you are training. There is no order involved, no formula, and you may or may not know what the population frame is until after you have finished your data collection. In addition, your sample might be biased, as it hasn't been randomly drawn, but you don't know whether it is. The sample may or may not be representative of the population. This happens, for example, when you test one training class and use the results to make decisions for an entire population of employees being trained.

2. A *quota sample* is used when something happens in your random sample and you need to replace a certain number of the sample, for example, to reach a certain percentage of the population. Perhaps individuals in your original random sample could not be used because they did not comply with program requirements, have dropped out, or can't be contacted when needed. You still need to have 10 percent of the population in the sample, so you

begin drawing names out of the hat until you end up with the correct number of respondents. Thus the sample (the original one with the new names added) may not be representative of the population, and your confidence in the sample is diminished.

3. A *purposive sample* is used when you greatly restrict the size of a population, or it is restricted for you because the subjects represent the informed group that you need. For example if you are gathering data on course development from military instructors, you are restricted to that informed group who have something to say on the matter and may use the entire population as your sample.

Sampling and Surveys

In recent years, surveys have become a popular method of gathering data, especially for accountability in such areas as health care and government. Surveys are only as successful as they are well planned and implemented. Planning includes selecting the best sampling technique for the job. Once again you are trying to select a number of subjects whose responses can be generalized for the target population. For example, in an attempt to determine the value of a particular family planning clinic in a community, a survey is sent out to all community members as determined by tax records. A population of five thousand is identified, so you draw a sample of five hundred to receive the survey.

Once the survey has been designed and administered, you will probably encounter the problem of nonresponse. You need to take some sort of action because anything under a 100 percent sample response means bias has entered into the results. That is, you cannot be sure if those who took the time to respond simply have a more favorable attitude toward the program than those who did not respond. What do you about it? You may need to make follow-up telephone calls to nonrespondents and ask some questions, such as why they did not choose to respond, whether the survey was too long or too difficult. You need to know whether the nonrespondent was negative to the treatment (the family planning clinic), to the data collection process (the survey), or to you (an evaluator). By doing this you try to ascertain whether those who did not respond are drastically different from those who did respond. You may need to use other follow-up procedures, such as e-mail, telephone, or another survey.

Putting It All Together

Our bias about evaluations is that they should be performed to assist the program staff in improving the program, and thus improving the product they deliver to the client. However, evaluators often find that they have other audiences to address, such as sponsors or parents, and other purposes for the results of the evaluation besides program improvement, such as deciding whether to consolidate funding behind one approach. Sometimes decisions need to be made about whether one direction, philosophy, or technique should be followed over another. These are difficult decisions to make because they may entail eliminating or adding programs, and thus eliminating or adding people's jobs. In such cases, decision makers like to have some hard data on which to rely. Hard data usually equate to a more rigorous evaluation design, or something that approaches research.

Questions and Exercise

Now that you have read Chapter Eight, return to the questions at the beginning of the chapter:

1. What are the differences between evaluation and research?
2. Why might an evaluator want to use a sample of individuals instead of all individuals?
3. What are the kinds of sampling?

Answer those questions in two ways:

- Write a general answer that applies to the chapter material.
- Use your new understanding to write a specific answer that applies to the scenario. Be sure to address these issues:

  In your opinion, will the Grandview staff be taking part in evaluation or research?

  Give three reasons to substantiate your answer.

  How does sampling figure into what they will be doing? Why do they need it, or why not?

Exercise

Once again, look back to Exercise I in Chapter One, in which you described a project of your own. Answer two questions:

1. Does my project represent research or evaluation? How do I make that decision?
2. Does my project involve sampling? If so, what type of sampling will I employ?

Further Reading

Graham, A. *Statistics*. Chicago: NTC/Contemporary, 1994.

McMillan, J. H. *Educational Research: Fundamentals for the Consumer*. New York: Harper Collins, 1992.

Norman, G. R., and Streiner, D. L. *PDQ Statistics*. (2nd ed.) St. Louis: Mosby, 1997.

Scriven, M. *Evaluation Thesaurus*. (4th ed.) Newbury Park, Calif.: Sage, 1991.

9

Writing the Evaluation Report

SCENARIO 9   The organizing committee for the Grandview gardening program knew that at the conclusion of the proposed gardening program, someone would have to write a report. The Cox Foundation required one. Beyond that obvious need, however, they wondered if there was any other reason for report writing. Everyone looked at each other, all thinking the same thing: "I really don't feel like writing another report. I do some form or other of reporting every day of the week!"

At this point, Ruth broke the silence. She said, "I'm sure that no one here needs or wants any extra work. But you probably remember that when I started this whole thing, the administration said that they would be delighted if I would do the legwork, but they would need to know what I was doing all along the way. They needed to keep their board of directors apprised." She concluded, "Don't we owe a report to the administration so that they can be prepared for the board?"

Mike Ramirez spoke up, "Ruth, I'm sure you're right. What does everyone else think?" The logic of Ruth's statements had, indeed, reached everyone at the meeting. Luis agreed, too, but he had been through a few evaluation experiences and still didn't feel that he understood the fine points of writing an evaluation report.

At this juncture, the voice from the corner of the room said, "Ask Judy Hallowell to write it!" Even as the group cheered the idea of having someone else do the job, they knew that Judy had been there to coach; she hadn't been hired to do the evaluation or to write the report.

Finally, Mike said, "What do you think about a compromise? We can call Judy and ask her to give us a few more hours of her time to at least get us going in the right direction on our evaluation report." Mike heard a unanimous "yes" to his suggestion. With that he concluded the meeting and went directly to the telephone to call Judy Hallowell.

Think about the following questions as you read Chapter Nine:

1. Do I need to write a final evaluation report?
2. For whom do I write the evaluation report?
3. What are the key components of the evaluation report?

When you finish reading, you should be able to answer the questions as they relate to the scenario as well as to the chapter material.

Key Words and Concepts

Interim evaluation report: A report, delivered either orally or in written form, written during the development or improvement of a program or project; done for the in-house staff

Summative evaluation report: A report written and delivered after the completion of a program or project for a funding agency, management, or other decision maker

Focus of the report: The chief concern of the audience for the report

Communicating Your Findings

All the efforts you have expended up to this point in designing and conducting the evaluation are of little consequence if you do not communicate the findings to the people who need it. Your reporting can be verbal or written, informal or formal, rough or polished. If you have completed only a formative evaluation, your reporting could be in the form of verbal comments provided to program staff during a staff meeting. However, the findings could also be written in a formal interim evaluation report that the program director could submit to the funding source. Although staff may expect interim reports, whether written or oral, federal grants frequently demand them in writing. A summative or final evaluation report is usually a written one and comes at the end of a program cycle.

Keep in mind that as the evaluator, you were appointed or hired by someone (that is, program director, funding agency, or others). You direct and submit your evaluation report to that person or entity. As a rule, if the sponsor has contracted you, write the report to address the sponsor's needs. If you were contracted by the program director or staff, write the report addressing their needs.

If you are writing an evaluation report for the program director, make it clear that this is primarily for his or her use. Many program directors will take your final evaluation report and submit it as their final report on the program to the sponsor. Program directors who know better will incorporate your report into their final report to the sponsor. Why? Because the evaluator's report is supposed to be objective in nature whether or not the evaluator is a part of the program. The findings may be supportive or critical of the program's operations. The program director needs to address the findings and attempt to explain them in the final report to the sponsor.

One more point about the evaluator's report: the data or information gathered can far exceed the scope of the evaluation, as you will see when you read the sample evaluation report at the end of the book. However, for the evaluation to be meaningful, the report must stick to the questions on which it was based.

Evaluation Reports

Most evaluations will call for a report that summarizes the history of the program as well as the goals, the methodology of the evaluation, findings, interpretations, conclusions, and recommendations. Summative evaluation reports need supporting tables, graphs, charts, or case studies that address targeted results. The important question that dictates the orientation of your reporting is, Who is your audience for the report? The answer provides you with a focus for your interpretations and recommendations. (See the Sample Evaluation Report for the Zoo in the Community program at the end of the book for an example.)

Depending on the evaluation audience (or focus), the style and length of the report will vary. An in-house evaluation to improve the way a program is implemented will require a different report from the summative evaluation report for a funding source.

Throughout the report preparation, the evaluator uses communication strategies that are appropriate to the decision-making audience. For example, before an in-house evaluation report reaches its final draft, your strategies might include circulating a draft report among staff or colleagues or participants with important findings that may or may not be included in the final report. The findings might be included in the draft in order to raise questions that go beyond the scope of the evaluation and to provoke future discussion (Wholey, Hatry, and Newcomer, 1994). Others' perspectives gleaned from responses to earlier drafts can even be included in the final draft.

How do you determine the focus of the report? The easiest way is to return to your evaluator's program description and the evaluation questions found there. If, for example, the funding agency wants to know the efficacy of having increased the funding by 10 percent, your report immediately has a focus. As illustrated in Table 9.1, the questions asked at the formative and summative evaluation stages in the program planning cycle, and the kinds of questions addressed in a comprehensive report, may help you to find one or more focal points for your audience. Sometimes you will need to write several different reports to address the needs, for example, of a funding agency, a school board, teachers, and parents.

The Report Outline

To stay organized, you can use an outline that will direct your report writing. Although it represents just one of several possible formats, the following list offers a reliable one. A discussion of each section follows. Note that the Zoo in the Community evaluation (the sample report at the end of the book) uses a slightly different and abbreviated format because it was prepared for the project director, who already had many of the facts regarding the history and background of the program.

OUTLINE OF AN EVALUATION REPORT

Suggested Organization	Section Title	Suggested Order for Writing the Sections
Section 1	Summary	Last
Section 2	Purposes of the evaluation	First
Section 3	Background information concerning the program	Second
Section 4	Description of the evaluation study and design	Third
Section 5	Results	Fourth
Section 6	Discussion of the program and its results	Fifth
Section 7	Conclusions and recommendations	Sixth

TABLE 9.1 Focus Points for Evaluation Reports.

Philosophy and Goals	Needs Analysis (Participants)	Program Planning	Program Implementation	Evaluation (For Yourself and Others)
FORMATIVE				
An agency may be looking at outcomes in terms of how they addressed their goals and objectives. Were the results in line with their mission statement?	How well did the program address the needs? To what extent has the program helped clients? What effect has the program had on the client system? (Can use satisfaction measures in the report.) Did procedures (activities) address specified needs of clients? Did the client needs change as they went through procedures?	Were procedures appropriate, planned to address needs? Did procedures include contingency plans? Did they allow for altering an activity or substituting a different one if necessary? Or starting a second class in the middle of the program, for example, to accommodate a manager?	To what extent was the program effectively or efficiently conducted? Did the procedures work efficiently and effectively? Did it go smoothly, leading to total implementation as scheduled?	Did the evaluation design look at the kinds of things the program needed to look at? Did it address the questions that needed to be addressed? Did the procedures collect appropriate data and in an appropriate way?
SUMMATIVE				
Were the procedures in line with acceptable program practices?	Did the results of the program significantly affect the client population? For		Did the results occur as a direct result of the activities, or can't you say that?	Did the evaluation address the hard questions that needed to be addressed? Did

any biases enter into the procedure? Did the evaluator help to change activities as the program went on?

Report on evaluator's effectiveness, evaluation's appropriateness, and the design's rigorousness. Could recommend alteration of any part of the design or recommendations of the evaluator.

Report on effectiveness of planned activities, efficiency of staff and the activities, and the extent of impact on clients. Can recommend alterations to activities, staff, staff development, or client preparation. (At what levels should clients be included or excluded from program?) Sponsors want these answers.

Report on the appropriateness of planned program and activities as well as meeting the needs of clients and the mission of the agency or organization. Answer this question: Did the program plan have an impact on both clients and agency? Recommend alterations of activities or the entire program as well as adoption or adaptation of activities.

example, did the program teach new managers to write?

Report on the extent to which outcomes and procedures fulfilled the needs of clients, regardless of the organization's goals.

REPORT

Report on the outcomes of program and whether outcomes were in line with program practices. Can recommend alteration of processes, of entire program, or of specific objectives or entire goals of agency.

Section One: Summary

As a brief overview of the evaluation report, this section summarizes the purpose of the evaluation, a history of findings from previous evaluations (if any), and lists major conclusions and recommendations. Designed for the person too busy to read the full report, the summary should be no more than one or two pages long. Although the summary should appear at the beginning of the report, it is written last so that the evaluator has the benefit of all interpretations, conclusions, and recommendations he or she will make.

Section Two: Statement of the Evaluation's Purpose

This section could be a few paragraphs or a chapter depending on your needs. It describes what the evaluation did and did not intend to accomplish. In effect, this section describes the assignment that the evaluator accepted, and as such it could probably be prepared immediately after the evaluator accepts the assignment. A draft of this statement can then be agreed upon by all interested parties and kept on file.

Section Two stems from the evaluator's program description and addresses the following questions:

Why was the evaluation undertaken?

What questions were asked?

Who sponsored (paid for) the evaluation or program?

Section Three: Background Information

This section sets the program in context, describing how the program was initiated and what it was supposed to do. If the evaluation audience consists of individuals who have no knowledge of the program, this section needs to be detailed. But if people who are familiar with the program will read the evaluation report, then Section Three can be a brief setting down of facts "for the record."

A draft of Section Three developed in the planning stages of the evaluation will ensure that the evaluator has a clear grasp of the program, including what is and is not supposed to be accomplished. The draft could then be circulated to program personnel for their comments. Typical content might address the following questions:

What was the origin of the program? (That is, what were the reasons for initiating the program?)

What are the standards and goals of the program?

What did the predecessor to this program look like? (What were its experiences and successes?)

Who makes up the program (faculty, trainees, and others)?

What are the characteristics of the program (materials, technology, and activities)?

Section Four: Description of the Evaluation Study

Section Four describes the methodology of the evaluation. The description includes the evaluation design for each evaluation question. In order to engender faith in the conclusions of the evaluation, you need to include every detail about how the information was obtained. Include a discussion of the evaluation model used (discrepancy, goal-free, or other), the sample, and the instruments, plus how you collected and analyzed the data.

Depending on the model you followed, the nature of the design reporting might change. For example, if you followed a goal-based model, your collection and analysis procedures would be described in terms of their aim at objectives presented in the program description or proposal. If, however, you were following a goal-free model, you would describe data collection instances and opportunities that arose during the evaluation. Interpretations and conclusions would be based on objective attainment for the goal-based model or on key accomplishments and shortcomings for the goal-free model.

A draft of Section Four should be written as the evaluation is being planned so that it can be circulated to the program personnel for their comments. Obviously, obtaining agreement beforehand about what will constitute a fair measure of the program will increase the credibility of the results.

Section Five: Results

This section presents the data that were collected from the various data sources. If the sources were reliable and valid, these become the "hard data" that people talk about. In addition, Section Five may include some "soft data" such as anecdotal evidence or testimonials about the program. Also include unexpected effects—things that staff did not anticipate but that nevertheless occurred.

The results section should be written after all the data have been analyzed for content (in the case of interviews), recorded in tables, graphed or plotted, and tested for significance where appropriate. Test scores are usually presented in tables showing means and standard deviations for each group. (See Appendix A for details.) Results of questionnaires are frequently summarized on a facsimile of the questionnaire itself.

Section Six: Discussion of the Program and Its Results

In the discussion section of the report, you want to interpret the evaluation findings. What do the findings say? What are the implications for clients, sponsors, staff? How did the results affect the students, trainees, or others?

Conceivably, Section Six could be included in Section Five along with information about the results. However, if the program or evaluation is quite complicated, it may be preferable to have a separate section for interpreting and discussing the results. The results should be discussed with particular reference to Section Two, the purposes of the evaluation. Also, here is where you, as the evaluator, have an opportunity to attempt an explanation of the findings—both positive and negative. Typical content includes answers to the following questions:

How good were the results of the program?

How did the program results compare with what might have been expected had there been no program?

How certain is it that the program caused the results?

Are there any other possible explanations of program results?

What were the costs associated with the program—dollar and nondollar (for example, the using up of resources or the loss of alternative opportunities)?

What were the benefits associated with the program—dollar and nondollar?

Either at the beginning or end of Section Six, if you can, provide a cost-benefit summary table in which both dollar and nondollar costs and benefits are listed. Distinguish operating costs from start-up costs, because the latter will not be incurred if the program is repeated. And be sure to distinguish costs and benefits for which the evaluation has produced sound evidence from suspected costs or benefits that have not been substantiated by objective procedures.

Section Seven: Conclusions and Recommendations

You may want to present this last section in the form of a list rather than in narrative form. Whatever the format, as evaluator you will advance recommendations for future steps, both short-term and long-term actions that will improve the program even further. Because this section is the most influential part of the report, you need to emphasize what is important and make clear what conclusions must be tentatively rather than firmly held. Take care, too, that this section attends to all the concerns raised in Section Two, which described in detail the purpose of the evaluation.

Some evaluators feel that they should not make recommendations at all but merely report evaluation data to decision makers. Others feel that the evaluator should make recommendations. In actual practice, the evaluator is frequently asked to make recommendations regarding the program or subsequent evaluations of the program or both. For example, should some instruments be modified or discarded for subsequent evaluations? Should a different design be used in a future evaluation?

The evaluator has an ethical responsibility to make explicit the value base upon which recommendations are made. For example, the evaluator who believes in the merits of the developmental view of learning might make different recommendations than one who advocates objectives-based instruction. More than likely, you were initially selected as the evaluator because of your expertise in both evaluation methodology and in the professional arena of the program, and the recommendations section is where you are really earning your money. Thus the contractor has an expectation that your recommendations for program improvement will be grounded in the best practices currently in the field. The evaluator, therefore, needs to clearly state the perspective from which recommendations are made.

The program planning team may also wish to make recommendations. Before writing this final section of the report, therefore, the evaluator might distribute copies of the results of the evaluation to the program staff. As a group, they can discuss the implications of the results with the evaluator, identifying those recommendations that are supported by the data. Both the staff's and the evaluator's recommendations can then be incorporated into this final section.

As a final caution, evaluators know that objectivity is crucial. Most evaluation reports will contain both positive and negative findings and sometimes findings that are not absolutely certain.

Events outside of the evaluation may obstruct or hinder the data collection. These events need to be included and explained fully.

Putting It All Together

A hard reality of the evaluation game is that as an evaluator, you are a "hired hand." As an external evaluator, you will downplay this point so that you have access to authentic and credible data. Objectivity is the goal and selling yourself as a professional who is performing a task that will benefit the program is key to a successful evaluation. Or, as an employee who works on the program, you may have another, "outside" role as the evaluator. For example, as you read in the Chapter Nine scenario, Judy Hallowell will not write the final report on the Grandview program. A Grandview staff member (or subcommittee) will do that. That person or entity will need to stress this outside role so that people will buy into the author's objectivity. Regardless of the model you follow, objectivity will make the evaluation results useful and credible to the audience.

Regardless of how credible and objective you become, however, if no one can read or understand your final reporting, you are ineffective as an evaluator. That reporting must be aimed at addressing questions that were posed early on by the staff, sponsors, or clients. You will be deemed a good evaluator according to your ability to address answers to those questions, keyed to the findings of the evaluation, in a format appropriate to the audience.

Questions and Exercise

Now that you have read Chapter Nine, return to the questions that you were asked to keep in mind at the beginning of the chapter.

1. Do I need to write a final evaluation report?
2. For whom do I write the evaluation report?
3. What are the key components of the evaluation report?

Answer those questions in two ways:

- Write a general answer that applies to the chapter material.
- Use your new understanding to write a specific answer that applies to the scenario. Be sure to address these issues:

   Were Ruth's concerns about writing a report for the administration legitimate ones?

   How do Ruth's concerns play right into the chapter's discussion of focus?

   Who are the other stakeholders interested in seeing the evaluation report?

Exercise

Take this final opportunity to write everything you know about the proposed gardening program on the evaluation design format in Exhibit 9.1. Feel free to "fill in the blanks" with appropriate decisions of your own.

Further Reading

Craig, D. P. *Hip Pocket Guide to Planning and Evaluation*. San Diego, Calif.: Pfeiffer, 1978.

Gray, S. T. *Evaluation with Power*. San Francisco: Jossey-Bass, 1998.

Patton, M. Q. *Practical Evaluation*. Newbury Park, Calif.: Sage, 1982.

Scriven, M. *Evaluation Thesaurus*. (4th ed.) Newbury Park, Calif.: Sage, 1991.

Zemke, R., and Kramlinger, T. *Figuring Things Out: A Trainer's Guide to Needs and Task Analysis*. Reading, Mass.: Addison-Wesley, 1982.

EXHIBIT 9.1 Evaluation Design Format.

Evaluation Question	Activities to Observe	Data Source	Population Sample	Data Collection Design	Responsibility	Data Analysis	Audience

Appendix:
More on Data Analysis

Note to the reader: In Chapter Seven, you may have found all that you need to know about working with data. We have included this appendix for those who need or want to delve more deeply into the subject.

Analyses for Each Level

Different statistics are used to measure central tendency, variability, and analysis of variance depending on the level of data you are dealing with (nominal, ordinal, interval, or ratio). As discussed in Chapter Seven, each level makes certain assumptions about the nature of the data, and these assumptions carry over to the types of statistical analyses appropriate for each.

Measures of Central Tendency

The central tendency is some point at which a data set is split in half. For nominal data that are primarily narrative responses and are often dichotomous variables (yes/no, male/female), the appropriate measure of central tendency (MCT) is the mode. The *mode* is the most frequently appearing response in the data set.

Ordinal data usually fits on a scale of some sort (such as responses ranging from Strongly Agree to Strongly Disagree) and the

MCT is either the median or the mode. The *median* is the midpoint in the data set or the value at which the data is split exactly in half.

For interval data, which have equal intervals separating each of the values in the response set (1, 2, 3, 4), and ratio data, which contain an absolute zero point, the appropriate MCT may be the mean, median, or mode. The *mean* is the arithmetic average of the scores in the data set.

Measures of Variability

Two sets of scores might have similar means, medians, or modes but be very different in the scatter of the scores in the data set. There is more variability in one set than the other. Therefore, you need a measure that illustrates the spread of these scores. The three most often used measures of variability (MV) are the range, interquartile, and the standard deviation.

For nominal data, the only appropriate MV is the range.

For ordinal data, the MV is the quartile deviation, explained in the following example. Let's say you are collecting data on participant perceptions of a computer literacy training session. The participants are asked to complete an evaluation instrument at the end of the training that asks a variety of questions on the session such as, "Were the objectives met? Was the trainer well prepared? Did the training meet your expectations?" Your instrument includes a Likert scale with these answer choices for each question: Strongly Agree (5), Agree (4), Neutral (3), Disagree (2), Strongly Disagree (1).

As the evaluator, you have been asked to analyze each of the questions separately to determine if there is any variability from one question to another. You compile all the responses from 100 participants over the course of four training sessions.

For the question, "Was the trainer well prepared?" the responses were Strongly Agree, 20; Agree, 40; Neutral, 5; Disagree, 20; Strongly Disagree, 15. You want to calculate the 75th percentile, that is, the score in the range of 1 to 5 where 75 percent of the scores fall below and 25 percent fall above. In this case, of the 100 respondents, 20 of them (20 percent) reported that they strongly agree with this statement. Another 40 (40 percent) indicate that they agree. Thus, the 75th percentile would fall in the Agree response category, for a score of 4.

Similarly, calculate the 25th percentile, the score in the range of 1 to 5 where 25 percent of the scores fall below and 75 percent above. In this case, 15 respondents (15 percent) reported that they strongly disagree with this statement. Another 20 (20 percent) indicate that they disagree. Thus, the 25th percentile would fall in the Disagree response category, for a score of 2.

Now, to calculate the interquartile deviation, subtract the 25th from the 75th percentile (4 – 2 = 2) and divide that by 2 (2/2 = 1). The interquartile deviation for this distribution of scores is 1.

What this means is that participants' scores on the question of preparation of the trainer tended to deviate by 1 response category. If you look at the response for this question that was selected by the greatest number of participants (Agree = 40 percent), or a response of 4, you can surmise that the majority of all responses fell within plus or minus one point of 4.

Like the range, the higher the number for the quartile deviation, the more the variability. The quartile deviation, however, is a more stable measure of variability.

For interval and ratio data, the standard deviation is used as the MV. The standard deviation is the most stable MV in that it takes into account each score in the data set.

Tests of Significance

At some point, an evaluator, like a researcher, will want to determine whether a certain treatment (for example, computer-based training) yields better results than another treatment or no treatment. The purpose is to ascertain that the difference in functioning between the two groups has more to do with a specific intervention than with chance. To statistically test this assumption, you can use a variety of tests of significance. For each of these statistical analyses, a number is generated which in turn is compared to an appropriate table of values to determine level of significance.

For nominal data, the most appropriate test is the chi-square (χ^2) test. This test relies on data that are in the form of frequency counts (actual counts or percentages that can be converted to frequencies) and on data that have categories (true categories) that are mutually exclusive. This test compares proportions actually observed with those that might be expected. These expected proportions represent one's best guess of what the proportions might look like if all things were equal. They may also be derived from previous experience or studies. The greater the difference between observed and expected results, the greater the chi-square value.

For ordinal data the appropriate test would be a sign test, Wilcoxon signed ranks test, or the Mann-Whitney U test. The sign test and the Wilcoxon could be used if you wanted to determine whether the functioning of individuals in one group at a point prior to treatment (pre) was statistically different than after the treatment (post). If the pre score for a person is higher than the post, then a minus sign (−) is assigned. If pre is the same as post, then a neutral sign (0) is assigned. If the pre score for a person is lower than the post, then a plus (+) sign is attributed. Consequently, it becomes the preponderance of one sign over the others that determines significance. Similarly, if you wish to determine whether the difference between the scores of individuals in two different groups is statistically significant, you could use the Mann-Whitney U test. In all three tests the pre and post scores, or the group 1 and group 2 scores, are compared and the differences (sign) are noted. All three tests and others are described in Seigel (1956).

For interval and ratio data, the appropriate test would be a t test. This test determines whether the means of two different groups are significantly different given a preselected probability level. The dependent t test would be used if you wanted to determine whether the functioning of individuals in one group from a point prior to treatment (pre) was statistically different from their functioning after the treatment (post). In this test, the mean is calculated for the entire data set. Then each score is subtracted from the mean. These differences are squared and added together (sum of squares). Then the data are used in a formula to determine the t value. This value is compared to a t-test table to determine significance.

A different test, the independent t test, would be used if you wished to determine whether the difference between the scores of individuals in two different groups was statistically significant.

Correlations

At some point in an evaluation, you may wish to assess to what degree a relationship exists between two or more variables. This does not infer a causal relationship as in the tests of significance, but just a relationship. The degree of relationship is calculated as a correlation coefficient and measured on a scale between -1.00 and $+1.00$. If two variables are highly correlated, you will see a correlation coefficient that is closer to 1.00 ($-$ or $+$) than to zero. If there is a weak correlation, the correlation coefficient will be closer to the zero.

For ordinal data, the appropriate correlation would be the Spearman rho. In this statistic, an inference is made that the data sets are rank ordered (for example, seniority at the time of training).

For interval and ratio data, the appropriate correlation would be the Pearson r. Like other measures at these data levels, the Pearson r uses each score in both distributions.

Significance Testing

One of the most powerful tools that evaluators and researchers have is the ability to infer causality by analyzing data. As discussed in Chapter Eight, the more rigorous the study and the more quantitative the data, the more you can employ formulas of statistical significance that will allow you to draw such inferences. To many people, the basic assumptions underlying significance testing are so difficult to grasp that they simply "take your word for it" and press their "I believe" button when using tests of statistical significance or reading the results. However, an understanding of the procedures will explain what the tests can really do and what they mean, so let us take a look at them.

Let's begin by talking about the normal curve. If you were to gather a set of scores and calculate the mean for those scores, you would assume that the scores below the mean and those above the mean would be evenly distributed. In other words, there would be a similar number of scores above and below the mean as illustrated in Figure A.1.

The second assumption, given what you have learned about the standard deviation, would be that 34 percent of the scores in the set fall on the minus side of the mean and 34 percent fall on the positive side of the mean. Or a total of 68 percent of the scores in the set should fall one standard deviation (SD) about the mean, as illustrated in Figure A.2.

Third, if you were to go out from the mean a second standard deviation, you could now account for an additional 13.5 percent of the scores on the minus side and 13.5 percent on the positive side of the mean. Thus, if you looked two standard deviations about the mean, you should account for 95 percent of the scores, as illustrated in Figure A.3.

FIGURE A.1 Normal Curve.

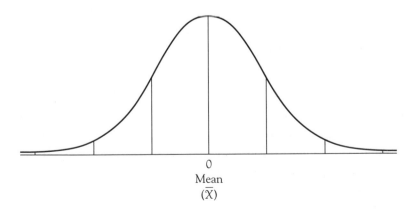

0
Mean
($\overline{X}$)

FIGURE A.2 Normal Curve and One Standard Deviation.

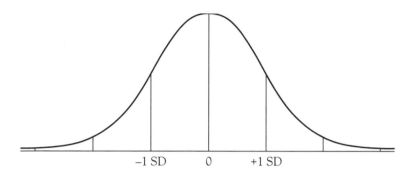

−1 SD   0   +1 SD

FIGURE A.3 Normal Curve and Two Standard Deviations.

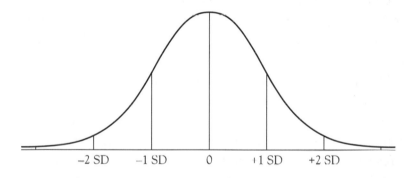

−2 SD   −1 SD   0   +1 SD   +2 SD

If you were to extend one more standard deviation you should account for 2 percent of the scores on either side of the mean or an additional 4 percent, for a total of 99 percent of the scores, as illustrated in Figure A.4.

Beyond three standard deviations you would be accounting for the remaining variance (0.05 percent below and 0.05 percent above the mean). The important point is the totals we have discussed: one standard deviation should account for 68 percent of the scores; two standard deviations should account for 95 percent of the scores, and three standard deviations should account for 99 percent of the scores. Statistical significance lies beyond the third deviation.

FIGURE A.4 Normal Curve and Three Standard Deviations.

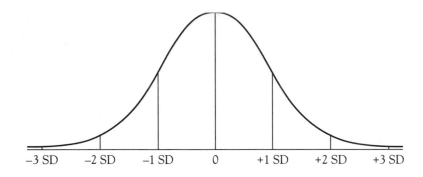

| −3 SD | −2 SD | −1 SD | 0 | +1 SD | +2 SD | +3 SD |

If the set of scores you possess is normally distributed, then the aforementioned proportions should hold. Put another way, if left purely to chance, the scores in your set should fall as we have described. If they do, there really is nothing remarkable or statistically significant about your set of scores.

However, if your distribution does not follow this pattern and many more scores fall into the range defined by four or even five standard deviations, then you have a distribution that is somewhat remarkable. Why? If your assumption is that 99 percent of the scores should fall within the four standard deviations about the mean, but many more than 0.05 percent fall in the fourth standard deviation range, then your distribution could not have been expected to occur simply by chance. Instead, the assumption is that something happened to cause those scores to fall outside of the expected distribution. This something, you would like to believe, was your program. This is where we get the .05 level of significance that is used to designate those findings of statistical analyses that are deemed statistically significant (or beyond chance occurrence).

This level of significance is constant regardless of the statistical analysis (t test, correlation coefficients, Wilcoxon test) and denotes a level of confidence that your findings were attributable to something more than chance. In some research a higher level of confidence is desirable, so the determination of significance is taken beyond the .05 level to the .01 or .001 levels, examining frequency even farther from the mean, to five or six standard deviations. However, the .05 level of significance is sufficient for most evaluation and research purposes.

Statistical and Practical Significance

Usually in an evaluation, you have neither the need nor the luxury to perform complex statistical analyses. If you can do so, it will contribute a great deal to the believability of your findings. Granted, you were appointed or hired because of your expertise and knowledge about the process, but having the "hard facts and figures" to back your anecdotal information and impressions will go a long way.

You do not necessarily have to be dismayed if, in conducting a test of significance on your data set, you find no statistically significant findings. At times there can be only practical significance to your findings. Take the example in Chapter Two of the evaluation of a high school career development program. In this program, the participating students attended academic classes three days of the school week and were given structured activities on job sites the other two days a week. At the close of the school year, participating and nonparticipating students were administered a standardized achievement examination. When the results were compared, there were no statistically significant differences between the posttest scores of the treatment and the control groups. In fact, the means of the two distributions were quite similar. At first glance, one would be moved to conclude that this Career Education Program was a failure. However, these career education students were in academic classes for only three days per week compared to the five days of the control students, a difference with significant implications for any evaluation. Yet they still achieved an equal level academically and also benefited from a wealth of work site experiences. Perhaps the Career Education Program did not help these students score higher academically, but it certainly didn't hurt them as they pursued their work-study agenda.

For more references on statistical analysis and for software, see the Further Reading and Software lists at the end of Chapter Seven.

Sample Evaluation Report

Following is an example of a final, or summative, evaluation report for a project in a city zoo. As you read through it, think about the following:

Who was the audience for this report?

Can you think of two other audiences that might want or benefit from either an oral or written report from the evaluator?

In this particular case, was the evaluator part of the program?

Once you have read the report, also consider the following question: What happens when there is more than one audience for the report, as is frequently the case? The evaluator may prepare multiple reports, using different reporting strategies for each audience. By gearing the style and content of the evaluation report to the audience, the evaluator increases the likelihood that the report will be read, and will influence people. For example, an evaluator might be asked to make a formal, written report to a funding agency, a school board, teachers, and parents. Whereas a highly technical and detailed report is appropriate for a funding agency, a leaflet-like summary that explains the highlights of the evaluation results in nontechnical terms may be more suitable for parents. The report to the school board might include a nontechnical section that presents major evaluation results plus a more technical report presented as an appendix.

ZOO IN THE COMMUNITY
FINAL EVALUATION REPORT
August 1993

CONTENTS

[ANNOTATION: *An evaluator may choose the format that suits his or her particular report. This is one possible format.*]

Introduction

Methodology

   Evaluation Design

   Instrumentation

   Analyses

Results

   Objectives

Recommendations

Appendices

   Appendix A: Self-Concept Questionnaire

   Appendix B: Semantic Differential

   Appendix C: Self-Evaluation Form

   Appendix D: Focus Group Questions

Introduction

[ANNOTATION: *Although an evaluation was mandated by the funding source, this report went first to the project director. In turn the project director sent parts of it along with her final report to the funding source.*] The Zoo in the Community project has been providing training to Providence-area teens and subsequent education to Rhode Island youth from several communities for the past six months. The project has been operating since February 1993 with the majority of time and effort in the early stage going to project start-up activities. The project was funded through grants from the Urban Parks and Recreation section of the National Park Service, The Rhode Island Foundation, and various private sponsors. The goal of the funding was to have the Park Zoo Docent Council develop and operate a project that would prepare disadvantaged and at-risk teens to be student activity leaders for the zoo as well as educate area elementary students as Junior Explorers in the link between science and the world of urban children. In order to address these ends there were three (3) foci of the Zoo in the Community project: First, identify and train the student activity leaders (SALs). Second, develop the educational activities to be used by the SALs. Third, provide those instructional activities to Junior Explorers (JEs), who were area elementary students participating in after-school child-care programs.

[ANNOTATION: *The introduction is brief and to the point. A long reiteration of history was not necessary because the report was going to a person who was in possession of the complete details.*]

To date the project staff have identified and trained the student activity leaders and completed two full cycles of educational activity with eight (8) groups of elementary students.

The project began in February 1993 and it completed activities in June 1993. This report, therefore, is a final evaluation of the Zoo in the Community project by an independent third party. The evaluation was designed by the third-party consultant in conference with the Zoo in the Community director. [ANNOTATION: *A third party, that is, an outside evaluator, was mandated by the funding source. The evaluator entered the process after activities were completed. Thus this is a summative report that looks at effectiveness. See Chapter One.*] The evaluation design collected data on the eight (8) objectives leading to the goal of the project for the purpose of examining overall project effectiveness. [ANNOTATION: *The reader of the report immediately knows the evaluation model—objective attainment—that was used. See Chapter Six.*]

This report will present a discussion of the data collected on a variety of aspects of project activity.

Methodology

The intent of Zoo in the Community is comprehensive in nature, allowing for zoo staff to train student activity leaders as environmental educators to develop self-esteem and leadership skills and master basic biological concepts in order to teach. In addition, Junior Explorers will gain ownership of the zoo as a place of learning and ownership of science as a lifelong interest.

It was important, therefore, that any evaluation of the Zoo in the Community project would take this comprehensive goal into account. The goal itself could not be evaluated but did provide the context for the evaluation design.

Evaluation Design

The evaluation design adopted by the evaluator and project director is based on an objective attainment model. However, in addition to these objectives the evaluation examined a number of other components of the center's operation.

The objectives of the project were as follows:

1. To build self-confidence in older youths (student activity leaders) by giving them positive experiences as teachers

2. To expose older youths (student activity leaders) to science and teach basic life science concepts in a new and meaningful context through real-world experiences

3. To provide practical training in teaching, technology, and handling scientific equipment to older youths

4. To demonstrate how the daily choices of urban youths affect both the local and global environment

5. To nurture inherent scientific interests in younger youths (Junior Explorers) by providing stimulating after-school experiences

6. To make younger youths (Junior Explorers) feel ownership of the zoo as a living laboratory where they are always welcome to learn

7. To bring exploration of the natural world and the basic concepts of ecology into the lives of urban youths

8. To integrate young people from diverse backgrounds by having disadvantaged urban youths (student activity leaders) teaching children (Junior Explorers) from various backgrounds

These objectives are both programmatic and behavioral in nature. They reflect actions and activities that were undertaken to both administer the project and identify impact(s) that the project might have had on Zoo in the Community participants. Therefore, the evaluation design allowed for data collection on the following evaluation questions:

- What specific methods and techniques were used by the project to recruit and train participants?
- What was discovered about effective methods of training student activity leaders?
- What effectiveness have these methods had on the student activity leaders and the Junior Explorers?

[ANNOTATION: *Evaluation questions were developed from the evaluator's program description. See Chapter Four.*]

Instrumentation

In order to collect information to be used in the evaluation, the evaluator visited the project site and interviewed project staff and participants. The purpose of these visits was to obtain perceptions and impressions from Zoo in the Community staff on how they set the project plan in motion and what they determined to be specific indicators of project success. The results of these interviews and a review of existing project records were used to help form an overall picture of the Zoo in the Community project.

Three instruments were also developed for the project. A self-concept questionnaire (Appendix A) was developed and used to collect self-esteem measures from the SALs on a pretest-posttest basis. A semantic differential (Appendix B) was developed and used to collect attitude toward science information from both the SALs and the JEs on a pretest-posttest basis. A self-evaluation form (Appendix C) was developed by project staff to collect baseline demographic and perceptual information from the SALs. [ANNOTATION: *The instruments listed here are qualitative measures. See Chapters One and Six.*]

Analyses

The results of the interviews and instrument administration were compiled and reviewed with respect to project objectives. The self-concept questionnaire, the semantic differential, and the self-evaluation form were all analyzed using a dependent t test. [ANNOTATION: *In* The ABCs of Evaluation, *see the Appendix for a discussion of* t *tests.*] This statistical procedure measures the extent of difference between two sets of matched scores from one population, to determine whether there is some reason to believe that pretest to posttest score differences across the population occurred as the result of some intervention instead of just happening by chance. In this instance the pretest responses of SALs to the self-concept questionnaire, the semantic differential, and the self-evaluation form were matched to their respective posttest responses. The pretest responses of the JEs to the semantic differential were matched to their respective posttest responses.

The staff interviews, SAL interviews, and focus group results were all analyzed for content and used to address or embellish discussion of specific objectives.

Results

This section of the report will cover the extent to which the project met its objectives.

Objectives

The Zoo in the Community project had identified eight (8) objectives for the project duration. These objectives formed the direction the project would take for the year and guided the project staff in monitoring all project activities. [ANNOTATION: *Discussion with the project director illuminated the objectives. Note that objectives guided decisions about data sources and activities. See Chapters Three and Four.*]

Data will be discussed for each objective.

Objective One: To build self-confidence in older youths (student activity leaders) by giving them positive experiences as teachers

To address this objective the project staff selected eight (8) student activity leaders to participate in the Zoo in the Community project. These high school students resided in the Providence area and represented an array of ethnic and racial groups. Prior to their being trained, the self-concept questionnaire was administered. [ANNOTATION: *This measure was written by staff to fit their particular needs.*] The instrument consisted of fifty-eight (58) items that required a response of either "Like me" or "Unlike me." The statements were mixed with both positive and negative orientations so that the individual had to read each item and respond uniquely rather than being able to respond in a single manner to each. Some items identify one as having a positive self-concept and some do not. The "positive" items are noted as appropriate responses and the instrument is scored measuring the total number of positive responses. Thus a total score of 58 indicates a very high (positive) self-concept, and conversely, a score of 0 indicates a very low (negative) self-concept. Because the purpose of this measure was not to identify or "pigeonhole" where an individual was, but instead to measure growth, the pretest-posttest analysis of group growth is the important one to note. The instruments were administered to all SALs; however, only seven (7) were correctly completed on a pretest and posttest basis. An analysis of the results are presented in Table 1.

[ANNOTATION: *In* The ABCs of Evaluation, *see the Appendix for a discussion of data analysis.*]

[ANNOTATION:

- *In Tables 1 to 3, "mean difference" refers to the total difference between the means (either pretest to posttest or one sample to another).*

- *"Degrees of freedom" refers to the number of valid subjects in the samples used with a reduction of either 1 ($n - 1$) or 2 ($n - 2$). This depends on the type of statistical test used or the type of comparison (pretest to posttest or one sample to another) and is usually stipulated in the formula.*

- *The value of t is the statistic calculated in a* t *test.*

TABLE 1 Dependent *t* Test of Student Activity Leaders' Self-Concept Questionnaire Results.

n	Mean Difference	df	t	p
7	1.29	6	.530	NS

Note: NS = not significant

- *The value of P (probability) shows whether the t statistic has been found to be statistically significant at the p < .01 or p < .05 level of significance.*]

A review of these scores indicates that the SALs had a wide range of scores on the self-concept questionnaire and some room for growth. However, both the size of the sample and the pretest to posttest changes within the group were not of a magnitude to be statistically significant.

To additionally examine the construct of self-confidence, the project director developed and administered a self-evaluation form that asked the SALs to respond on a five- (5) point scale relative to their perceived level of skill and confidence in sixteen (16) areas. These skill ratings were totaled, giving a total score to be used in a pretest-posttest analysis of growth. Thus a total score of 80 indicates a very high overall self-rating for skill, and conversely, a score of 16 indicates a very low overall self-rating for skill. An analysis of the results of this administration is presented in Table 2.

A review of these skill ratings indicates that the SALs have a wide range of scores on the self-evaluation form. However, again both the size of the sample and the pretest to posttest changes within the group were not of a magnitude to be statistically significant.

During the exit interview the SALs were asked, "What did you learn about yourself?" The responses indicate that by and large the SALs learned quite a bit about their ability to deal with younger children. Some commented that before the project they were rather short with and intolerant of younger children. However, given the

TABLE 2 Dependent *t* Test of Student Activity Leaders' Self-Evaluation Results.

n	Mean Difference	df	t	p
7	7.71	6	1.69	NS

training and experience of Zoo in the Community, they found that they could be patient and not lose their temper in the face of bombardment with questions and highly active behavior. Some reported that they were getting along better with their younger siblings and other children in the neighborhood. The overall comments elicited by this question indicated that the SALs did learn something about themselves and their capabilities, limits, and strengths through interacting with the JEs. [ANNOTATION: *See Chapter Six for a discussion of the interview, a qualitative evaluation technique.*]

Based on these observations, it is determined that although the project did not statistically improve the self-concept of the SALs as measured by the self-concept scale and the self-evaluation instruments, it did help the SALs to feel better about and learn something about themselves.

Objective Two: To expose older youths to science in a new and meaningful context through real-world experiences

Once all SALs were selected, the project director began a training program that simultaneously provided information on the zoo and on instructional styles and activities that are appropriate with younger students. As part of the training, the director, with the SALs, developed the curriculum and activities to be used over the four (4) sessions with each of the JE groups.

The activities were separated into two areas—Wetlands Ecology and Evidence of Animals. The Wetlands Ecology unit had the SALs guide the JEs through a series of activities to collect water samples and identify species in the samples. Discussions were generated about the types of species found in the samples and their relationships with other environments. The electronic tracking of animals in the wild was also discussed.

The Evidence of Animals unit had the SALs play a twenty-questions kind of game where the JEs would examine evidence and try to identify the animal. Also, a skeleton of a sea lion was used to help the JEs identify different bone structures and their proximity to one another.

The common denominator in the two units was problem solving. The JEs were required to connect pieces of evidence, elaborate on findings, extrapolate information into other settings, and think about their environment as a community of living organisms.

Questions that the JEs asked the SALs over the course of the project suggested that these JEs had not thought much about the types, variety, and amount of wildlife that exist in their neighborhoods. Also, their questions indicated that there were species of animals they were encountering for the first time.

As a result of these observations, it is determined that this objective was met.

Objective Three: To provide practical training in teaching, technology, and handling scientific equipment to older youths

Part of the training that the project staff gave to the SALs included the identification and use of several complicated measuring devices. The water sample collecting and study required the use of such equipment. Also, in their indoctrination to the myriad of zoo units and departments, the SALs became acquainted with the machinery that keeps a zoo going. A feeling shared by most of the SALs was that they would have liked more information and training on more areas of the zoo operation. The use of sophisticated equipment was, at first, intimidating to them. However, as they developed confidence, their curiosity was also piqued. [ANNOTATION: *Stakeholders sometimes suggest the direction in which projects will go in the future.*]

As a result of these observations, it is determined that this objective was met.

Objective Four: To demonstrate how the daily choices of urban youths affect both the local and global environment

The curriculum that the SALs and the director developed included information not only on the animals housed at the zoo but also on how people affect the lives of these animals. Also, a great deal of stress was placed on how these animals are beneficial to people's lives and to the planet. Often urban youths disassociate an urban lifestyle from that of animals in the wild. The Zoo in the Community project attempted to bring these two worlds back together for the SALs.

During exit interviews, the SALs reported that they had learned quite a bit about the animals housed at the zoo and how they can live in harmony with people. Several reported that it was "fun" to learn something new every day about animals and nature. Several expected to be working hands-on with the animals and were disappointed when this did not occur to a larger degree. In addition, several of the SALs would have liked to learn more about the museum at the zoo.

Objective Five: To nurture inherent scientific interests in younger youths by providing stimulating after-school experiences

To measure this objective, a semantic differential was administered to both the SALs and the JEs. The instrument consisted of fourteen (14) adjective pairs that were responded to on a five (5) point scale separating the pairs. The statements were mixed, alternating the positive and negative orientations of the pairs so that the individual had to read each item and respond uniquely rather than being able to respond in a straight-line (thoughtless) manner to each. Individuals were asked to mark a point on the scale corresponding to how they felt about the word at the top of the instrument—in this case "science." Those responses were scored from 1 to 5 (1 being the negative adjective and 5 being the positive), and the instrument was scored measuring the total number of responses given. Thus a total score of 70 indicated a very positive attitude and conversely, a score of 14 indicated a very negative attitude. As with the self-concept questionnaire, the purpose of this measure was not to identify or pigeonhole where an individual was but to measure growth, so the pretest-posttest analyses of growth were the important ones to note.

Although instruments were administered to all participants in the project (both SALs and JEs), only seven (7) SALs and thirty-six (36) JEs correctly completed the instrument to make their results usable. An analysis of the results of the administration of this instrument to the SALs and JEs is presented in Table 3.

[ANNOTATION: *In The ABCs of Evaluation, see the Appendix for an explanation of how data from qualitative instruments is analyzed.*]

A review of these statistical analyses indicates that the SALs showed a statistically significant gain on the semantic differential from pretest to posttest. This is in line with the original goal of the Zoo in the Community project to change youths' attitude toward science.

However, the JEs' pretest to posttest score changes were not statistically significant. A review of the raw scores of the pretests and posttests indicated that the JEs tended to have high scores in the pretest (mean = 61.4) and that posttest scores (mean = 62.5) were not much higher. This would suggest that the JEs had positive attitudes toward science at the outset, leaving little room for improvement.

Based on these measures, it is determined that the project accomplished this objective of improving the attitude toward science of the SALs, but did not improve on the already positive attitude of the JEs.

Objective Six: To make younger youths feel ownership of the zoo as a living laboratory where they are always welcome to learn

TABLE 3 Dependent *t* Test of Student Activity Leaders (SALs) and Junior Explorers (JEs) Zoo in the Community Semantic Differential Pretest-Posttest Scores for "Science."

Group	n	Mean Difference	df	t	p
SAL	7	4.43	6	3.0	.0241*
JE	36	1.917	35	1.4	.1697**

*$p < .05$

**Not statistically significant

Focus groups were conducted with the SALs by a docent (volunteer) who had some evaluation background. Two focus groups were conducted—each with four (4) of the SALs. One group had the sixteen- and seventeen-year-old SALs, and the other group had the fifteen- and sixteen-year-olds. The questions asked in the focus groups covered a range of topics including level of involvement in project activities, what was learned, and suggested improvements. A list of the focus group questions appears in Appendix D.

The SALs felt that their Zoo in the Community experience was quite beneficial. All reported that they learned a lot about the zoo and about the animals and their habitats. All SALs, except those who were graduating, wanted to return to the Zoo in the Community project next year and several would have liked to remain employed over the summer.

Although the SALs did feel that the Zoo in the Community project was their project, the majority did not feel that the zoo staff treated them as regular members of the staff. Several SALs reported that various zookeepers disliked or felt uncomfortable around them. Other zoo staff treated them like kids or stereotyped them as "punks." The most vehement complaint of the SALs was that the zoo gift shop clerk would not grant them the employee discount.

Unfortunately, no focus group or data collection was performed as part of this evaluation to examine the perceptions of the JEs on this question of "ownership." This is definitely a point that needs to be added to any future evaluation of the Zoo in the Community project.

Given a review of the focus group results with the SALs, this evaluator must conclude that the SALs did develop a feeling of "ownership" for the zoo as a learning laboratory. However, they did not develop an overall feeling of ownership of or kinship with the zoo in general. But as this was not a result of any actions by zoo staff who were directly related to the Zoo in the Community project or the education unit, it is the conclusion of this evaluator that this objective was achieved. No comments can be made on the development of a feeling of ownership on the part of the JEs.

Objective Seven: To bring exploration of the natural world and the basic concepts of ecology into the lives of urban youths

The essence of the Zoo in the Community project was to target urban youth and acquaint them with the workings of the natural world. As reported earlier, the SALs were extensively trained in these notions and have used the new awareness in developing instructional materials and activities and in teaching groups of JEs. As reported in the focus groups and the evaluator's exit interview with the SALs, they were quite appreciative of this newfound resource in their backyard and had a better understanding of how to use it. [ANNOTATION: *See Chapter Six regarding interviewing.*]

The JE groups learned about a variety of natural world topics beyond a superficial glance at a picture in a book or magazine. The SALs helped them to think about the natural world from a variety of perspectives. The educational activities not only provided them with information about different animals that are in the zoo but also gave these children a new perspective on the place of animals in their world.

Given the review of these data, this evaluator must conclude that this objective was achieved.

Objective Eight: To integrate young people from diverse backgrounds by having disadvantaged urban youths teaching children from different backgrounds

[ANNOTATION: *This narrative shows the project moving through its life cycle, from this objective, through activities, to selection of measures (focus sessions, exit interviews, and survey), to the evaluator's final conclusion.*]

The main activity of the Zoo in the Community project was the training of urban teens as SALs who would then conduct structured educational activities with urban youths as JEs. As reported earlier, this was accomplished. The SALs were recruited and trained; instructional activities were developed and materials prepared; JE groups were recruited and scheduled into two sessions of five weeks each; and educational activities were conducted by the SALs.

This objective was measured using two postproject focus group sessions with SALs, exit interviews, and a review of project records. The results of the focus group sessions and evaluator exit interviews indicated that the SALs learned a great deal about working with young children. The SALs reported that patience was something they had not believed they had but that it quickly emerged as they fielded questions, coordinated activities, managed the learning "chaos," and dealt with learners who were excited about a topic. The SALs felt that they were learning as they were teaching. The more experience they received with the JEs the better they felt about their instructional abilities. With more time came more patience, responsibility, ability to talk with the JEs, structuring of appropriate questions, realization that some of the JEs were smart, and insight into how to use that intelligence in the group.

Comments received from the chaperones who accompanied the JE groups were quite complimentary of the SALs.

- "(SALs) were great with the kids and seemed to hold the children's attention, which is sometimes difficult."
- "They (SALs) were very good. Any time you can get teens these days to do for others, you have done something."
- "Well organized."
- "They were well prepared and patient, and the children enjoyed all aspects."
- "Excellent. Very patient and put across information that kept the children's attention. The communication they had with the children was great."

Given the review of the focus group, interview, and survey data, this evaluator must conclude that this objective was achieved.

Overall Results.   After reviewing all project records, interviewing project staff, and examining instructional activities, this evaluator must conclude that the Zoo in the Community project successfully attained all eight (8) of the project's objectives.

Recommendations

[ANNOTATION: *The project director may include some of these recommendations in her own report to the funding source. See Chapter Nine.*]

It is important that the Zoo in the Community project receive funding to continue beyond FY93 because the operation of the project to date indicates that it is a welcome and much needed resource for Rhode Island urban after-school day-care students. Consequently, this evaluator will make several recommendations to help the Zoo in the Community staff plan for future directions. However, it is important to note that the project, as implemented, operated in a commendable fashion. During its short operating time, Zoo in the Community managed to provide many hours of education to many Rhode Island after-school day-care students. [ANNOTATION: *The recommendations are very useful in that they give suggestions—specific activities—for moving forward whether or not this funding continues. Clearly, the recommendations are for the project director and should not go directly to the funding source without careful review on her part.*]

Recommendation One: SALs need to be treated as regular zoo staff.

The major negative comments from SALs involved the manner in which they felt other Zoo staff treated them. The SALs said that the staff (not the Zoo in the Community staff) treated them as "kids," "punks," or "second-class citizens." Perhaps an orientation session, an open communication to all staff, an individual introduction, even a staff name badge might suffice to get other zoo staff to begin treating the SALs in an appropriate manner.

Recommendation Two: The Zoo in the Community development process should not be dismantled for lack of funding but instead expanded into other service areas and marketed to projects sponsored by other funding sources.

The Zoo in the Community staff have designed a process of training and activity development that provides effective and expedient zoo-related education to after-school day-care agencies and students. Over the past five months, a relatively brief period, the Zoo in the Community staff trained SALs, designed activities, and operated two sessions of education for JEs. This represents an instructional process that is quite effective and might be useful to other units of the zoo. Perhaps SALs could work in the museum, with the special exhibits, or in the main office. An underlying purpose of Zoo in the Community is career education, and there are other careers to be investigated at the zoo.

Recommendation Three: Publicity, in any shape, can only help to increase awareness of the Zoo in the Community project and possibly open some new avenues of resources and funding.

It would be advisable to use success stories of instances where the Zoo in the Community has resulted in a significant change in a person's or family's life, career, or emotional state as the basis for published reports in appropriate professional periodicals and local newspapers. These changes could be on the part of the SALs or the JEs. These stories would inform the general public and the profession of the success of Zoo in the Community and the impact it has had on people's lives. Both types of publicity can only help to increase awareness of Zoo in the Community and possibly open some new avenues of resources.

Recommendation Four: The instructional sessions should be scheduled for longer periods or lengthened and spread over more sessions.

Suggestions from SALs and chaperones who participated in Zoo in the Community sessions indicated that although the sessions were well received and appreciated, too much information was squeezed into too little time. This would indicate that either the sessions were designed to present far more information than the time allotted or too much time was used in discussion so that the full session curriculum could not be completed. Comments of participants indicate that the latter is not the case; therefore the format of sessions should be reexamined. The distribution of time among preparation, instruction, and clean-up and debriefing was appropriate, but the amount of time for instruction could be extended.

Recommendation Five: Develop beginner, intermediate, and advanced levels for the instructional offerings to accommodate both the novice and the well-trained JE.

Zoo in the Community has only operated for half a year, but during that time staff have seen different levels of need from the JE groups. Some of the JEs were well informed about the zoo upon entry and were "bored" with the activities, whereas others were fascinated. All the day-care centers indicated a willingness to participate again in the project by bringing new JEs and also the same JEs again. Thus there is probably a market for repeat participants. These repeaters are likely to want something more advanced than the same elementary information. This might even be another answer to marketing Zoo in the Community to other zoo units (horizontally) and to more in-depth examination of certain topics (vertically).

[ANNOTATION: *The recommendation gets into totally new territory; here the evaluator proposes repeat participation and marketing to other zoo units, and later suggests recognizing diversity with a bilingual approach.*]

Recommendation Six: If the Zoo in the Community project is refunded for fiscal year 1994 operation, an autumn start would result in a much more efficient and effective project that would probably amass impressive service delivery statistics, given the project's track record.

If the project begins early in the fall so that SALs are recruited and trained early and fall/winter activities can begin on time, there could be at least four and possibly as many as six sessions of activities. This schedule would accommodate the various levels of activity recommended earlier and the possible increase in the number of JE participants.

Recommendation Seven: Sessions could be offered in other languages with an SAL who is bilingual.

Perhaps a session could be developed and offered in a language other than English. Many urban youths are foreign born and have limited English-speaking ability. Such sessions would open the zoo to a much wider population.

Recommendation Eight: JE groups should be better oriented.

During the early sessions the SALs spend a great deal of time orienting the JEs to the rules, behavior, and activities of the project. Perhaps this should be performed prior to the JEs' first session. Either an orientation package could be developed and distributed or an SAL might visit a center and talk to the children prior to their first visit to the zoo.

Recommendation Nine: The maturity level of SALs could be examined as part of the selection process.

Some SAL comments indicated that future SALs should be at least sixteen years old because the younger ones were less committed to working and to the concept of holding a job. They had problems with taking the job seriously, regular and timely attendance, and commitment. However, the project intended (as a side effect) to increase the maturity of participants. Maturity level did improve as SALs evolved in their role. Evidently some of the SALs felt that for certain of their colleagues, this evolution was not enough.

Recommendation Ten: The role and responsibilities of the SALs should be expanded.

The SALs had a number of good ideas about project improvements, next steps, and ways of managing the project. These ideas included thoughts about new activities, ways the SALs and JEs interact, other areas of the zoo to involve, structure of the instructional teams, use of chaperones, and additional SAL training. These ideas all represented a common theme—the SALs had adopted the Zoo in the Community project as their own and were ready to improve and expand on it. This enthusiasm should be harnessed and used.

Recommendation Eleven: The educational impact of the project for Junior Explorers needs to be examined.

The project showed that it was a worthwhile endeavor for its impact on the SALs. However, the impact on the JEs (that was measured this year) was not evident. Perhaps the evaluation next time could include a component that examines the cognitive growth of both JEs and SALs. [ANNOTATION: *This recommendation shows that there may be new ground to cover with a slightly different scheme for data collection.*]

APPENDIX A

Self-Concept Questionnaire

NAME _____ DATE _____

If the statement describes how you usually feel, put a check (√) in the column "Like me." If the statement does not describe how you usually feel, put a check (√) in the column "Unlike me." There are no right or wrong answers.

	Like me	Unlike me
1. I spend a lot of time daydreaming.		
2. I'm pretty sure of myself.		
3. I often wish I were someone else.		
4. I'm easy to like.		
5. My parent(s) and I have a lot of fun together.		
6. I never worry about anything.		
7. I find it very hard to talk in front of the class.		
8. I wish I were younger.		
9. There are lots of things about myself I'd change if I could.		
10. I can make up my mind without too much trouble.		
11. I'm a lot of fun to be with.		
12. I get upset easily at home.		
13. I always do the right thing.		
14. I'm proud of my schoolwork.		
15. Someone always has to tell me what to do.		
16. It takes me a long time to get used to anything new.		
17. I'm often sorry for the things I do.		
18. I'm popular with kids my own age.		
19. My parent(s) usually consider my feelings.		
20. I'm never unhappy.		
21. I'm doing the best work that I can.		
22. I give in very easily.		

Like me   Unlike me

23. I can usually take care of myself.
24. I'm pretty happy.
25. I would rather play with kids younger than me.
27. I like everyone I know.
28. I like to be called on in class.
29. I understand myself.
30. It's pretty tough to be me.
31. Things are all mixed up in my life.
32. Kids usually follow my ideas.
33. No one pays much attention to me at home.
34. I never get scolded.
35. I'm not doing as well in school as I'd like to.
36. I can make up my mind and stick to it.
37. I really don't like being a boy or girl.
38. I have a low opinion of myself.
39. I don't like to be with other people.
40. There are many times when I'd like to leave home.
41. I'm never shy.
42. I often feel upset in school.
43. I often feel ashamed of myself.
44. I'm not as nice looking as most people.
45. If I have something to say, I usually say it.
46. Kids pick on me very often.
47. My parent(s) understand me.
48. I always tell the truth.
49. My teacher makes me feel I'm not good enough.
50. I don't care what happens to me.
51. I'm a failure.
52. I get upset easily when I'm scolded.
53. Most people are better liked than I am.

	Like me	Unlike me

54. I usually feel as if my parent(s) are pushing me.
55. I always know what to say to people.
56. I often get discouraged in school.
57. Things usually don't bother me.
58. I can't be depended on.

APPENDIX B

Semantic Differential

NAME _____ AGE _____

DIRECTIONS

Below you will find a list of words with opposite meanings. Between each of these pairs of words there are five spaces. Please place a check mark (√) in one of the five spaces to show how you feel about the word at the top of the list.

Here is an example:

WAR

GOOD	/__ /__ /__ /__ /✓ /	BAD
DESTROY	/✓ /__ /__ /__ /__ /	SAVE

In this example, a check mark has been placed to show how someone would show if they thought that WAR was *very bad* and *very destructive*.

Please be sure to make only one check mark for each pair of words. Also, please do not skip any pairs of words.

SCIENCE

BORING	/__ /__ /__ /___ /__ /	EXCITING
NICE	/__ /__ /__ /__ /__ /	AWFUL
GOOD	/__ /__ /__ /__ /__ /	BAD
UNINTERESTING	/__ /__ /__ /__ /__ /	INTERESTING
QUICK	/__ /__ /__ /__ /__ /	SLOW
SAD	/__ /__ /__ /__ /__ /	HAPPY
DEAD	/__ /__ /__ /__ /__ /	ALIVE
PROUD	/__ /__ /__ /__ /__ /	ASHAMED
GO TO	/__ /__ /__ /__ /__ /	STAY AWAY FROM
NOT HELPFUL	/__ /__ /__ /__ /__ /	HELPFUL
STRONG	/__ /__ /__ /__ /__ /	WEAK
DULL	/__ /__ /__ /__ /__ /	ENTERTAINING
PARTICIPATE	/__ /__ /__ /__ /__ /	NOT PARTICIPATE
FAIR	/__ /__ /__ /__ /__ /	UNFAIR

APPENDIX C

Self-Evaluation Form

Zoo in the Community
Self-Evaluation Form

NAME _____ DATE _____

The following are skills that would be helpful in working at the zoo. Give yourself a rating from 1 (not skilled in this area) to 5 (highly skilled in this area).

Responsibility	1	2	3	4	5
Punctuality	1	2	3	4	5
Patience	1	2	3	4	5
Self-discipline	1	2	3	4	5
Humor	1	2	3	4	5
Being organized	1	2	3	4	5
Communicating clearly	1	2	3	4	5
Being involved in my work	1	2	3	4	5
Working well with kids	1	2	3	4	5
Working well with coworkers	1	2	3	4	5
Accepting differences in others	1	2	3	4	5
Creativity	1	2	3	4	5
Enthusiasm	1	2	3	4	5
Self-respect	1	2	3	4	5
Honesty	1	2	3	4	5
Ease with animals	1	2	3	4	5

APPENDIX D

Focus Group Questions

1. How useful was the second training week?
2. What else would you have liked to see in the second training week?
3. How burned out do you feel after working here for four months? Do you still have the same amount of energy? What do you think about working here for ten months?
4. What were your expectations of working at the zoo?
5. Would you have liked to learn more about the zoo? If so, what areas?
6. Did you enjoy working at the zoo?
7. Was the ratio of SALs to younger kids good enough? Could you have handled more kids? Fewer kids? Was it the right number?
8. How did it work having four SALs team-teach? Too many people? Too few?
9. Describe the interaction of after-school chaperones with the groups.
10. Would you change the curriculum units you were teaching? Add different components? Use the zoo more? Less?
11. Do you have general suggestions or comments for next year?
12. Did you feel like you were a member of the zoo staff?
13. How did the structure of the individual days work, with a thirty-minute prep, one hour with kids, and a thirty-minute cleanup? Was this enough time, too little time, too much time for each?
14. Did you want more responsibility? If so, in what areas could you have taken more responsibility?
15. What do you think of the idea that one group of SALs would travel to after-school centers to teach?

16. Did the time of the program (3:15–5:15) work with your school schedule?

17. What do you think about having every Friday as a training day?

18. How else could we have used this training day?

References

Babbie, E. *The Practice of Social Research*. (5th ed.) Belmont, Calif.: Wadsworth, 1989.

Eisner, E. W. *The Enlightened Eye: Qualitative Inquiry and the Enhancement of Educational Practice*. (2nd ed.) New York: Merrill, 1997.

Fink, A., and Kosecoff, J. *An Evaluation Primer Workbook: Practical Exercises for the Health Professional*. San Francisco: Sage, 1978.

Gatewood, R. D., and Feild, H. S. *Human Resource Selection*. New York: Harcourt Brace Jovanovich, 1994.

Gay, L. R. *Educational Research: Competencies for Analysis and Application*. (5th ed.) New York: Merrill, 1995.

Gray, S. T. *Evaluation with Power*. San Francisco: Jossey-Bass, 1998.

Kirkpatrick, D. L. *Evaluating Training Programs*. San Francisco: Berrett-Koehler, 1994.

Madaus, G. F., Scriven, M., and Stufflebeam, D. L. (eds.). *Evaluation Models: Viewpoints on Educational and Human Services Evaluation*. Boston: Kluwer-Nijhoff, 1983.

McMillan, J. H. *Educational Research: Fundamentals for the Consumer*. New York: Harper Collins, 1992.

Popham, W. James (ed.). *Evaluation in Education: Current Applications*. Berkeley, Calif.: McCutchan, 1974.

Provus, M. *Discrepancy Evaluation*. Berkeley, Calif.: McCutchan, 1971.

Quinones, S., and Kirshstein, R. "An Educator's Guide to Evaluating the Use of Technology in Schools and Classrooms." [http://www.ed.gov/pubs/EdTechGuide]. Dec. 1998.

Rivlin, A. M. *Systematic Thinking for Social Action*. Washington: Brookings Institution, 1971.

Rossi, P. H., and Freeman, H. E. *Evaluation: A Systematic Approach*. Newbury Park, Calif.: Sage, 1993.

Scriven, M. *Evaluation Thesaurus*. Newbury Park, Calif.: Sage, 1991.

Seigel, S. *Nonparametric Statistics for the Behavioral Sciences*. New York: McGraw-Hill, 1956.

Wells, S. E. (ed.). *Horticultural Therapy and the Older Adult Population*. New York: Haworth Press, 1997.

Wholey, J. S., Hatry, H. P., and Newcomer, K. E. (eds.). *Handbook of Practical Program Evaluation*. San Francisco: Jossey-Bass, 1994.

Williams, B. *A Sampler on Sampling*. New York: Wiley, 1978.

Index

A

ABE. *See* Adult basic education project
Accountability, 28–29
Activities, as part of design format, 18
Adult basic education project (ABE), 74, 75
Adult learning center (ALC), 74, 75
Adversary evaluation model, 78, 79
ALC. *See* Adult learning center
Antecedent data. *See* Data sources: and existing data
Art criticism evaluation model, 77, 79
Audience, in evaluation design format, 17

B

Baldrige Award, 29
Benchmarks, 14
Benefits, potential, derived from evaluation: and increased knowledge of outcomes, 25–26; and opportunities presented, 25; to sponsors and staff, 24–25
Bias, avoiding, 96
Branching process, in interviews, 94, 95, 99

C

Cause-and-effect relationship, establishment of, 129
Center for the Study of Evaluation, 50

Central tendency, measures of (MCT): and calculation of mean, 112, 156; concept of, 108; in data analysis, 110–113; and median measure, 112–113, 155–156; mode measure in, 111–112, 155–156
Change, and stages of evaluation, 14
Chi-square test, 158
Clients, monitoring movement of, 39
Coding, 109
Composite data, 92
Consumer's Report, 73
Consumer's Union, 73
Convenience sample, 130
Correlation coefficient, 159
Correlational research, experimental research *versus*, 130
Cox Foundation, 2, 22, 23, 139
Craig, D. P., 152
Credibility, of evaluator, 27–28
Cumulative scale, 99

D

Data: four levels of, 88–90; and interval data, 90; and nominal data, 88–89; and ordinal data, 89–90; and ratio data, 90
Data analysis: and evaluation design format, 19; levels of data in, 116–121; measures of central tendency in, 110–113; measures of variability in, 113–116; overview of, 108–109; and statistics, 110

Data collection: four levels of data in, 88–90; nature of, 90–91; sources for, 87–88

Data collection design, 18–19

Data sources: and existing data, 91–93; identification of, 86–87; and interviews, 94–98; and newly collected data, 93; and observational analysis, 103–104; as part of design format, 18; and scales, 98–100; and sentence completion, 100–101; and standardized tests, 101–103

Decision-making evaluation model, 76, 79

Department of Labor. *See* United States Department of Labor

Discrepancy evaluation model, 71–73, 79

E

Educational Research: Fundamentals for the Consumer (McMillan), 138

Effectiveness: definition of, 3; evaluation of, 5–8; questions of, in a formal mandated evaluation, 11–12

Efficiency: definition of, 3; evaluation of, 5–8; questions of, in a formally mandated evaluation, 11–12

Eisner, E. W., 77

EPD. *See* Evaluator's program description

Equal appearing intervals, 98–99

Evaluation: of alternatives, 8; common denominators in, 3–4; design format for, 16; of effectiveness of the program, 9–10; formal reasons for, 10–13; and formative *versus* summative evaluations, 14; and identification of areas for improvement, 8–9; of impact on the participants, 9–10; of participant impressions, 9–10; practical application of, 13–14; and program cycles, 14–19; and return on investment for the organization, 8–9; two definitions of, 4–5

Evaluation, considerations about: and decision-making needs, 29–30; and research purposes, 30; and social and political atmosphere, 27–29

Evaluation: Methods for Assessing Program Effectiveness (Weiss), 84

Evaluation consumers, 28

Evaluation design format, 65–66, 78, 80–82, 106, 124

Evaluation Models: Viewpoints on Educa-

tional and Human Services (Madaus, Scriven, and Stufflebeam), 84

Evaluation questions, as part of design format, 17–18

Evaluation report: background information to, 146–147; as communication of findings, 141; conclusions and recommendations list in, 149–151; and description of study, 147–148; and discussion of program and results, 148–149; focus of, 142, 144–145; outline of, 143–151; and results of findings, 148; and statement of purpose, 146; strategies for, 142–143; summary section of, 146

Evaluation Thesaurus (Scriven), 138, 152

Evaluation with Power (Gray), 152

Evaluator's program description (EPD), 38, 70, 87; and data sources, 87; development of, 57–58; general purpose of, 58; for Pharmacy Training Program, 61; and rapport with program staff, 63; sample dialogue for, 58–60; as starting point for evaluation, 62–63; uses of, 55–57

Ex post facto design, 130

Experimental, *versus* correlational research, 130

F

Fair Labor Standards Act of 1938, 42

Federal grants, 5

Feild, H. S., 88, 95

Figuring Things Out: A Trainer's Guide to Needs and Task Analysis (Zemke and Kramlinger), 105, 123, 152

Fitz-Gibbon, C. T., 123

Fixed alternative questions, 95

Forced choice scales, 98

Formative evaluations: activities for, 49; concept of, 35; and program implementation, 45–46; *versus* summative evaluations, 14

Freedman, D., 123

Freeman, H. E., 4, 28, 35, 74

Funnel questions, 95, 96

G

Gatewood, R. D., 88, 95

Gay, L. R., 98

Generizability, concept of, 126

Goal-based evaluation model, 76–78, 79
Goal-free evaluation model, 73–75, 79
Graham, A., 123, 138
Gray, S. T., 22–23, 58, 83, 152

H

*Handbook in Research and Evaluation: A
   Collection of Principles, Methods, and
   Strategies* (Isaac and Michael), 84
Hatry, H. P., 5, 36, 74, 87, 103, 142
*Hip Pocket Guide to Planning and Evalua-
   tion* (Craig), 152
How to Calculate Statistics (Fitz-Gibbon
   and Morris), 123
*How to Use Qualitative Methods in Evalua-
   tion* (Patton), 123
Hypothesis, concept of, 68

I

Impact: definition of, 3; evaluation of,
   5–8; importance of, in behavior or
   attitude modification, 25–26
Information, and possible limitations of
   evaluation, 25–26
Inland Revenue Department (United
   Kingdom), 63
International Organization for Standardization (ISO), 77, 96
Interval data: and analysis, 119; concept
   of, 86; and levels of data collection, 90
Interviews: kinds of questions found in,
   95–96; and semistructured interview,
   94; and standardized interview schedule, 94; and unstructured interview,
   94–95
Isaac, S, 84
ISO. *See* International Organization for
   Standardization

J

Judgment sample, 135

K

Kirkpatrick, D. L., 9
Kirshstein, R., 62
Kramlinger, T., 105, 123, 152

L

Likert scale, 98
Limitations, of evaluation, 26–27

M

Madaus, G. F., 75–77, 84
Management information systems (MIS),
   39
Mandate, 10–11
Mann-Whitney U test, 158
McMillan, J. H., 87, 138
Michael, W., 84
Minnesota Multiphasic Personality
   Inventory (MMPI), 102
MIS. *See* Management information
   systems
Models for evaluation: and adversary
   model, 78; and art criticism model, 77;
   and choosing a model, 78–80; and
   decision-making model, 76; and discrepancy evaluation model, 71–73;
   and goal-based model, 76–78; and
   goal-free model, 73–75; overview of,
   68–71; and systems analysis model, 77;
   and transaction model, 75
Monitoring, 14; concept of, 35; of job-
   training program, 40–41; and process
   of monitoring, 38–43; sample data
   types for, 41–43
Morris, L. L., 123

N

Needs analysis: activities for, 48; in
   program planning cycle, 43–44
Newcomer, K. E., 5, 35, 74, 87, 103,
   142
Nominal data: and chi-square test, 158;
   concept of, 86; and levels of data collection, 88–90
Nonprobability sampling methods: and
   judgment sample, 135; and purposive
   sample, 136; and quota sample,
   135–136
Normal curve, 160; and one standard
   deviation, 161; and three standard
   deviations, 161–162; and two standard
   deviations, 161
Norman, G. R., 123, 138

O

Objective attainment model. *See* Goal-based evaluation model
Open-ended questions, 95
Ordinal data: concept of, 86; and levels of data collection, 89–90; and Wilcoxon and Mann-Whitney U tests, 158
Outcomes: definition of, 25; increased understanding of, 25–26
Owens, 77

P

Patton, M. Q., 123, 152
PDQ Statistics (Norman and Streiner), 123, 138
Personnel evaluation, 9
Pisani, R., 123
Planning, 29–30
Policymaking, 29–30
Popham, W. J., 73
Population, concept of, in data collection, 126
Population sample, as part of design format, 18
Positive termination, 39
Practical Evaluation (Patton), 152
Probability sampling methods. *See* Random sample
Product evaluation. *See* Summative evaluation
Program cycles, 36–38; and formative evaluation, 45–46; and needs analysis, 43–44; and program implementation, 45–46; and program phases, 36–38; and program planning, 44; and role of stakeholders, 35–36; and summative evaluation, 46
Program planning: activities for, 48–49; in program life cycle, 44
Program planning cycle, 34, 56
Project cycles: *See* Program cycles
Provus, M., 71
Public records: as data sources, 91–93; privacy and confidentiality issues around, 92
Purposive sample, 136
Purves, R., 123

Q

Qualitative methodologies: and coding, 109; concept of, 68, 70; and data collection techniques, 87; and descision-making model, 76; and goal-based model, 77; and goal-free model, 75; and research, 130–131
Quantitative methodologies: concept of, 68, 70; and data collection techniques, 88; and decision-making model, 76; and goal-based model, 77; in research, 130–131
Quartiles, 114–115
Quinones, S., 62
Quota sample, 135–136

R

Random sample: and cluster random sample, 134; concept of, 126; and multi-stage random sample, 134–135; and simple random selection, 133–134; and stratified random sample, 134; and systematic random sample, 134
Ranges, 114–115
Ratio data: and analysis, 121; concept of, 86; and levels of data collection, 90
Research: conditions of, 129–130; determining, from intent, 126–128; versus evaluation, 69–70; and evaluation design, 128–130; and nonprobability sampling methods, 135–136; and probability sampling methods, 133–135; qualitative or quantitative data in, 130–131; sampling in, 131–133; and surveys, 136–137
Research, as reason for evaluation, 30
Resource, concept of, 23
Responsibility, and evaluation design format, 19
Rossi, P. H., 4, 28, 35, 74

S

Samples: concept of, 126; and nonprobability sampling methods, 135–136; and probability sampling methods, 133–135; and sampling in research, 131–133; and surveys, 136–137
SAS Institute, Inc., 123

Scale items, 95
Scriven, M., 44, 73, 75–77, 84, 138, 152
Search committees, 8
Semantic differential scale, 100
Significance, tests of, 157–163
Significance testing, 159–163
SPSS, Inc., 123
Stake, R. E., 75
Stakeholders: concept of, 23; role of, in
    program cycles, 35–36
Stamp, J., 63
Standard deviation, 115–116
Standards, concept of, 24
Statistical analysis, 163–164
Statistics: and data analysis, 109–110;
    concept of, 108
Statistics (Freedman, Pisani, and Purves),
    123
Statistics (Graham), 123, 138
Streiner, D. L., 123, 138
Stufflebeam, D. L., 75–77, 84
Subjectivity, and transaction model, 75
Summative evaluation: activities for, 49;
    concept of, 35; formative versus, 14; in
    program cycle, 46
Surveys, 136–137
Systems analysis model, 77, 79

T

Transaction model, 75, 80
Trivia, focus on, 27

U

United States Department of Labor, 41

V

Value-laden words, 96
Variability, measures of (MV), 108,
    156–157; quartiles in, 114–115; range
    in, 114–115; and standard deviation,
    115–116; and variance, 116
Variance, 115–116

W

Weiss, C. W., 84
Wells, S. E., 1
Wholey, J. S., 5, 36, 74, 87, 103, 142
Wilcoxon signed ranks test, 158, 162
Williams, B., 133

Z

Zemke, R., 105, 123, 152